T0312018

Cambridge Elements ≡

Elements in Law, Economics and Politics

Series Editor in Chief
Carmine Guerriero, *University of Bologna*

Series Co-Editors
Rosa Ferrer, *UPF and Barcelona GSE*
Nuno Garoupa, *George Mason University*
Mariana Mota Prado, *University of Toronto*
Murat Mungan, *George Mason University*

THE STRATEGIC ANALYSIS OF JUDICIAL BEHAVIOR

A Comparative Perspective

Lee Epstein
Washington University in St. Louis
Keren Weinshall
Hebrew University of Jerusalem

CAMBRIDGE
UNIVERSITY PRESS

CAMBRIDGE
UNIVERSITY PRESS

University Printing House, Cambridge CB2 8BS, United Kingdom

One Liberty Plaza, 20th Floor, New York, NY 10006, USA

477 Williamstown Road, Port Melbourne, VIC 3207, Australia

314–321, 3rd Floor, Plot 3, Splendor Forum, Jasola District Centre,
New Delhi – 110025, India

79 Anson Road, #06–04/06, Singapore 079906

Cambridge University Press is part of the University of Cambridge.

It furthers the University's mission by disseminating knowledge in the pursuit of
education, learning, and research at the highest international levels of excellence.

www.cambridge.org
Information on this title: www.cambridge.org/9781009048859
DOI: 10.1017/9781009049030

First published 2021

A catalogue record for this publication is available from the British Library.

ISBN 978-1-009-04885-9 Paperback
ISSN 2732-4931 (online)
ISSN 2732-4923 (print)

The Strategic Analysis of Judicial Behavior

A Comparative Perspective

Elements in Law, Economics and Politics

DOI: 10.1017/9781009049030
First published online: May 2021

The co-editors in charge of this submission were Nuno Garoupa and
Carmine Guerriero.

Lee Epstein
Washington University in St. Louis

Keren Weinshall
Hebrew University of Jerusalem

Author for correspondence: Keren Weinshall, keren.weinshall@mail.huji.ac.il

Abstract: The past decade has witnessed a worldwide explosion of work aimed at illuminating judicial behavior: the choices judges make and the consequences of their choices. We focus on strategic accounts of judicial behavior. As in other approaches to judging, preferences and institutions play a central role but strategic accounts are unique in one important respect: They draw attention to the interdependent – i.e., the strategic – nature of judicial decisions. On strategic accounts, judges do not make decisions in a vacuum, but rather attend to the preferences and likely actions of other actors, including their colleagues, superiors, politicians, and the public. We survey the major methodological approaches for conducting strategic analysis and consider how scholars have used them to provide insight into the effect of internal and external actors on the judges' choices. As far as these studies have traveled in illuminating judicial behavior, many opportunities for forward movement remain. We flag four in the conclusion.

This Element also has a video abstract: www.cambridge.org/judicialbehavior

Keywords: hierarchy of justice, judicial preferences, legal institutions, rational choice, separation of powers

ISBNs: 9781009048859 (PB), 9781009049030 (OC)
ISSNs: 2732-4931 (online), 2732-4923 (print)

Contents

1 Introduction

The analysis of judicial behavior is thriving. Once the sole province of US scholars – and mostly political scientists at that – researchers throughout the world are illuminating how and why judges make the choices they do and what effect those choices have on society.[1]

Guiding work on judicial behavior is a range of theories, reflecting different disciplinary traditions, as Table 1 shows. But common features of these accounts are not hard to spot. First, all ascribe a key role to the judges' preferences. This is obvious for the attitudinal model under which judges vote in accord with their ideological commitments. Preferences also figure into the labor market model, which draws attention to personal motivations for judicial choices; and for legalism, which holds that adhering to the law is an end in and of itself. Identity accounts and thinking-fast judging are less focused on any one set of goals but they help explain why judges hold particular preferences (identity approaches) and why, no matter how hard they try, judges may be unable to maximize them (thinking-fast judging).[2]

A second common feature of the approaches is that they highlight the importance of institutions – or rules that shape judicial choices. For the legal model, formal constitutional provisions, laws, precedent, and the like serve as guideposts for judges desiring to follow the law (Eskridge, 1991a; Knight, 1992; Knight and Epstein, 1996a). Identity approaches show how particular rules allow personal characteristics to seep into the judges' choices, such as those making transparent the litigants' religion, race, and ethnicity (Shayo and Zussman, 2011). Even the attitudinal model, although often caricatured as "judges vote on the basis of their ideology," appreciates the importance of institutions. Judges only enjoy "enormous latitude to reach decisions based on their policy preferences" when they can serve for life on a court of last resort and when that court has substantial control over the cases it will hear and decide (Segal and Spaeth, 2002).[3] For judges operating under these rules, the labor market approach concurs on the importance of ideology (Epstein, Landes, and Posner, 2013; Alarie and Green, 2017).

As Table 1 makes plain, preferences and institutions are also central to strategic accounts of judicial behavior – the subject of this Element. But strategic analysis adds a third ingredient: interdependency. In strategic accounts, judges do not make decisions in a vacuum, but, rather, attend to

---

[1] Worth noting, however, is that some of the pioneers of US judicial behavior conducted the first systematic comparative studies (e.g., Schubert and Danelski, 1969; Becker, 1970; Tate, 1971). See Dyevre (2010).

[2] We return to thinking-fast judging in Section 6.

[3] These are just some of the factors that can lead to (more or less) ideological voting. For others, see Section 2.1.1.

Table 1 Six approaches to the study of judicial behavior

Approach (disciplinary origin(s))	Description
Attitudinal model (political science, psychology)	Judges' votes reflect their ideological attitudes toward case facts[4]
Legalism (strong version) (law)	Judges "find" the meaning of legal rules through politically neutral methods[5]
Thinking-fast judging (psychology, behavioral economics)	Judges rely on heuristics, intuitions and the like to make fast decisions without much effort[6]
Identity accounts (psychology, sociology)	Judges' biographies, personal characteristics, and identities affect their choices[7]
Labor market model (economics)	Judges are motivated and constrained by (mostly) nonpecuniary costs (e.g., effort, criticism) and benefits (e.g., esteem, influence, self-expression)[8]
Strategic accounts (economics, political science)	Judges are strategic actors who realize that their ability to achieve their goals depends on the preferences of other actors, the choices they expect others to make, and the institutional context in which they interact[9]

the preferences and likely actions of other key players, including their colleagues, judicial superiors, politicians, and the public.

---

[4] Segal and Spaeth, 2002.

[5] Under a weaker version of legalism, "law" (broadly defined) constrains judges from acting on their personal preferences, intuitions, biases, and emotions. Because this version – "law-as-an-institution" – figures prominently in strategic accounts, we consider it in Section 2.3.

[6] See, generally, Kahneman, 2011; Thaler, 2015. Numerous experiments on judges show that nonrational factors complicate their ability to make (strategically) rational decisions (Rachlinski et. al., 2009; Rachlinski, Guthrie, and Wistrich, 2011; Sonnemans and van Dijk, 2012; Wistrich, Rachlinski, and Guthrie, 2015). Observational studies include Shayo and Zussman, 2011; Epstein, Parker, and Segal, 2018; Eren and Mocan, 2018; Segal, Sood, and Woodson, 2018.

[7] Examples include national identity (Posner and de Figueiredo, 2005; Voeten, 2008), race (Cox and Miles, 2008; Kastellec, 2013; Sen 2015), gender (Boyd, Epstein, and Martin, 2010; Haire and Moyer, 2015), and religion (Sisk, Heise, and Morriss, 2004; Shayo and Zussman, 2011).

[8] See, e.g., Posner, 1993, 2008; Alarie and Green, 2017.

[9] From Epstein and Knight, 1998a.

Strategic accounts of judging, in short, contain three essential components: (1) judges' actions are directed toward the attainment of goals; (2) judges are strategic or interdependent decision makers, meaning they realize that to achieve their goals, they must consider the preferences and likely actions of other relevant actors; and (3) institutions structure the judges' interactions with these other actors.

In what follows, we explore the literature on the forms of strategic behavior in courts around the world and the ways in which preference-maximizing judges interact with important players in their society. Section 2 provides a foreword to strategic analysis, fleshing out its three components: judicial preferences (including policy, personal, and institutional goals), the institutional context, and the interdependencies between judges and other relevant actors. In Section 3, we survey the major methodological approaches for conducting strategic analysis; and Sections 4 and 5 consider how scholars have used those method-ologies to provide insight into the effect of internal and external actors on the judges' choices. The conclusion flags opportunities for future research.

2 Building Strategic Accounts

Strategic accounts consist of three components: preferences, interdependency, and institutions. Because the three are foundational in any strategic analysis, each merits attention.[10]

2.1 Preferences

Strategic accounts assume that people make decisions consistent with their goals and interests. We say that judges (or anyone else for that matter) make rational decisions when they choose a course of action that they believe satisfies their desires most efficiently. To give meaning to this assumption – essentially, that judges maximize their preferences – we researchers must identify the judges' goals. If we do not, our explanations become tautological because we can always claim that a judge's goal is to do exactly what we observe her doing (Ordeshook, 1992).

On several accounts of judicial behavior, the judges' motivations are fixed; for example, the attitudinal model holds that judges pursue policy goals and only policy goals (Segal and Spaeth, 2002); so too strong versions of legalism suggest that judges' sole goal is to follow "the law." Strategic accounts, in contrast, enable researchers to advance any motivations they believe judges hold. And scholars have taken advantage of this flexibility, positing three classes of motivations – policy, personal, and institutional

---

[10] We do not recount the history of the strategic analysis of judicial behavior because other reviews exist (Cameron, 1993; Epstein and Knight, 2000; Epstein and Jacobi, 2010).

motivations – although, as we hasten to note, analyses can consider all three simultaneously by, say, weighting motivations in the judges' utility function (Knight and Epstein, 1996b; Epstein, Landes, and Posner, 2013), among other approaches (see, generally, Helmke and Sanders, 2006).

2.1.1 Policy

Many early strategic studies characterized judges as "single-minded seekers of policy" (George and Epstein, 1992, 325), a phrase encapsulating the idea that judges work to bring the law in line with their preferred policy position (Murphy, 1964; Pritchett, 1961; Rohde, 1972; Eskridge, 1991a, b; Spiller and Gely, 1992; Cross and Tiller, 1998; Epstein and Knight, 1998a). By policy position, scholars usually mean the judges' ideological preferences (although to assess these preferences, scholars use both partisan and ideological measures. More on this point soon.)

The emphasis on ideology continues today in large part because scholars have offered plausible (although somewhat distinct) reasons and mounds of data for thinking that ideology affects the choices judges make. That certainly holds for US justices (Segal and Spaeth, 2002; Epstein, Landes, and Posner, 2013; Baum, 2017) but they are hardly unique: In virtually all studies that measure it, the judges' partisanship or ideology has a role to play. Work on the Norwegian Supreme Court by Grendstad et al. (2015), for example, establishes that justices appointed by social democratic governments are significantly more likely than nonsocialist appointees to find for the litigant pursuing a "public economic interest." Ideology (as measured by the appointing regime) plays a bigger role in these decisions than most any other factor that Grendstad et al. considered. Hönnige (2009) shows that ideology helps predict the votes of judges serving on the French and German constitutional courts (see also Hanretty, 2012); and Carroll and Tiede (2012) identify dissent patterns on the Constitutional Court of Chile "consistent with a general separation between the judges with center-left and right backgrounds." In their study of Spanish Constitutional Court judges, Garoupa, Gomez-Pomar, and Grembi (2013, 516) report that under certain conditions, "[t]he personal ideology of the judges does matter," leading the authors to "reject the formalist approach taken by traditional constitutional law scholars in Spain." Likewise, Coroado, Garoupa, and Magalhães (2017) persuasively demonstrate that the Portuguese Constitutional Court's decisions on austerity policies are less a function of business cycles than of policy preferences.

We could go on; many other studies of courts around the globe reach similar conclusions (Weiden, 2011; Weinshall-Margel, 2011; Dalla, Escresa, and Garoupa,

2014; Kantorowicz and Garoupa, 2016). At the same time, however, these studies demonstrate that ideological (or partisan) motivations pose their share of difficulties.

One follows from the ways that scholars assess empirically the judges' policy positions. Sometimes they use partisan measures (e.g., the appointing regime's party, the judges' partisan identity, or even their campaign contributions); and sometimes they deploy ideological measures (e.g., those derived from voting patterns or from text analysis of opinions or pre-appointment newspaper editorials).[11] For this reason, research on judicial behavior tends to treat political goals, policy goals, ideological goals, and partisan goals as interchangeable. Setting aside theoretical qualms about conflating these terms,[12] empirically all the various measures of policy preferences operate under assumptions that are worrying, unacknowledged, or both. Assessing judges' ideology on the basis of their votes, for example, assumes that votes are mainly ideologically driven. Likewise, partisan measures assume that policy preferences motivate voting aligned with party identity, when, in fact, those patterns may be a manifestation of strategically motivated behavior, especially on courts in which judges are attentive to the implications of their decisions for their future career prospects.

A second difficulty, a limit really, of ideological (or partisan) motivations is that no matter the study, their explanatory power may be constrained by high levels of consensus on courts worldwide. True, socialist appointees on the Norwegian Court, relative to nonsocialists, are more inclined to support public economic interests. But with a unanimity rate of about 80 percent, the opposing Norwegian partisans are mostly allied (Bentsen, 2019). More generally, for many apex courts, the effect of ideology is less pronounced than it is in the US Supreme Court[13] (Weinshall, Sommer, and Ritov, 2018); and even in the US, moving down the judicial hierarchy from apex to trial courts, ideology and partisanship carry even less weight (Hettinger, Lindquist, and Martinek, 2006; Zorn and Bowie, 2010; Boyd and Sievert, 2013; Epstein, Landes, and Posner, 2013).

---

[11] For a review of these measures, see Epstein et al., 2012; Weinshall, Sommer, and Ritov, 2018 and Bonica and Sen, 2021.

[12] The literature on political behavior shows that, however closely connected ideology and partisanship, they are distinct concepts, resulting in distinct behavior. In other words, a meaningful difference exists between "partisan loyalists" and "policy loyalists" (for a review, see Barber and Pope, 2019).

[13] Then again, even the US Supreme Court – a highly "political court" (Alarie and Green, 2017) – issues unanimous decisions in 40 percent of its cases, meaning that the most extreme liberals/Democrats and conservatives/Republicans often find common ground.

Why? The list of explanations for the varying strength of ideology is long and now includes the process of judicial appointments (e.g., the more political actors involved or the more contentious the process, the more political the court) (Wetstein et al., 2009; Robinson, 2013), as well as agenda-setting mechanisms (Eisenberg et al., 2012; Alarie and Green, 2017), the size of the court's docket (Narayan and Smyth, 2007), and the size of judicial panels (Weinshall et al. 2018) – such that courts with a mandatory docket, high caseload, and fluid or small panels tend to be more legalistic. The multidimensional nature of legal issues and the limitations of ideological proxies may also contribute to weaker (observed) connections between policy preferences and voting.

Regardless of the precise reasons for the differential effect of "political preferences," the upshot is this: However useful partisanship and ideology are for understanding judicial behavior, they are not the only motivations at work (and they may not even be especially important for many judges). Fortunately, strategic accounts allow scholars to posit others.

2.1.2 Personal Preferences

As the pool of scholars studying judicial behavior has grown to include economists, psychologists, and legal academics, and the targets of inquiry have expanded to include judges throughout the world – many of whom are more career-minded than politically oriented – increasing attention has been paid to personal motivations for judicial choice (Helmke and Sanders, 2006; Garoupa and Ginsburg, 2015; Melcarne, 2017). The idea is that, given time constraints, judges seek to maximize their preferences over a set of personal factors (some of which also have implications for political and institutional goals) (see, generally, Helmke and Sanders, 2006; Epstein and Knight, 2013). Examples include: job satisfaction (Shapiro and Levy, 1995; Drahozal, 1998; Baum, 2006; Engel and Zhurakhovska, 2017);[14] promotion to a "higher" or more prestigious job or office (Salzberger and Fenn, 1999; Ramseyer and Rasmussen, 2001; Melcarne, 2017); leisure (Klein and Hume, 2003; Clark, Engst, and Staton, 2018);[15] salary

---

[14] Job satisfaction is usually conceived in positive terms: as the judges' internal satisfaction of feeling that they are doing a good job, as well as the more social dimensions of judicial work, such as relations with other judges, clerks, and staff. de Figueiredo, Lahav, and Siegelman (2019), however, reveal the negative side of job satisfaction. The authors demonstrate how fear of public shaming causes US district court judges to swiftly resolve "old" cases and motions to avoid publication in the Six-Month List (a twice-yearly public list detailing the judges' backlogs). The swift resolution comes at the price of delays in cases for which the deadline is less pressing.

[15] Such that, at some point, "the opportunity cost of foregone leisure exceeds the benefits to the judge of additional time spent making decisions" (Drahozal, 1998, 476).

and income (Cooter, 1983; Toma, 1991; Melcarne, 2017);[16] and external satisfactions that come from being a judge, including reputation, prestige, power, influence, and celebrity (Miceli and Cosgel, 1994; Baum, 1997, 2006; Schauer, 2000; Dothan, 2015; Garoupa and Ginsburg, 2015).

This class of personal preferences has two especially nice properties. First, because all the elements are rather universal motivations, they lend themselves to comparative analysis. Second, even though personal preferences derive from parametric (nonstrategic) rational choice models of judicial behavior,[17] they are useful for strategic analysis. That is because maximizing personal preferences almost always requires judges to account for the preferences and likely actions of others, whether colleagues or external actors.

The desire for promotion illustrates both properties. Enhancing future job prospects could seem to be an important factor influencing the personal utility that judges gain from their work: It tends to increase job satisfaction, prestige, reputation, and salary.[18] For this reason, it is no surprise that many studies provide evidence of a connection between the judges' choices and career-advancement goals. In the USA, for example, federal judges with some realistic possibility of promotion impose harsher sentences on criminal defendants to avoid being tagged as soft on crime by appointing authorities (and the public) (Epstein, Landes, and Posner, 2013). Likewise, these "auditioners" are more likely to vote in line with the preferences of the president who could promote them (Black and Owens, 2016). The same holds in Japan where judges tend to defer to the national government because deference improves their chances of "doing better in their careers" (Ramseyer and Rasmussen, 2001). Along somewhat different lines, Italian Constitutional Court judges (who serve for a nine-year nonrenewable term) make judicial choices designed to enhance their post-court professional opportunities (Melcarne, 2017); and UK judges work to avoid reversal because a lower reversal rate increases their prestige, in addition to the likelihood of promotion (Salzberger and Fenn, 1999).

2.1.3 Institutional Preferences

In general, institutional preferences implicate the interest of government actors in their relative power and authority (Knight and Epstein, 1996b). When it

---

[16] That is, all else equal, judges, like most of us, prefer more salary, income, and personal comfort to less.

[17] Specifically, personal motivations grow out of the labor market approach introduced by Posner (1993, 2008) and interrogated empirically in Epstein, Landes, and Posner (2013) and Alarie and Green (2017).

[18] Promotion also could be coincident with policy preferences: The higher judges sit in the hierarchy, the more important the cases they hear and the greater the opportunity to influence the law.

comes to courts, usually lacking "influence over either the sword or the purse" (Hamilton, 1788), institutionalist judges care about issuing decisions that the public and the ruling regime will respect and implement (Epstein, Knight, and Shvetsova, 2002), while avoiding institutional sanctions that would undermine their court's legitimacy (Helmke and Sanders, 2006; Clark, 2011). Possible sanctions that could be imposed against judges and their courts are many in number and severity, ranging from impeachment, removal, and court-packing to criminal indictment, physical violence, and even death (Rosenberg, 1992; Helmke, 2005).

Hints within the literature suggest that institutional preferences are strongest when a court is seeking to establish itself as a player within a regime and/or for the court's leader (e.g., chief justice or president) (Katz, 2006; Fettig and Benesh, 2016; Li, 2020). Maybe so. But the literature provides plenty of examples of judges on well-established courts giving less weight to personal and political preferences in an effort to maintain and even deepen their court's legitimacy (Dothan, 2015). Krehbiel (2016), for example, demonstrates how the German Constitutional Court (a highly respected court) strategically uses hearings to generate public support for its decisions and, ultimately, to increase the odds of government compliance. Another example is the tendency of Israeli justices to intervene latently in security policy by promoting court settlements in the days following deadly terror attacks, compared with openly accepting petitions against the security forces in times of peace (Hofnung and Weinshall-Margel, 2010).

These are but a few of the strategies institutionalist-oriented judges deploy to accomplish the twin goals of issuing efficacious decisions and avoiding sanctions. We consider others in Section 5, which explores interactions between courts and external actors – many of which are driven by the judges' institutional preferences.

2.2 Interdependent (Strategic) Decision Making

The second part of the strategic account is tied to the first: For judges to maximize their preferences, whatever they may be, they must act strategically. By "strategic," we mean that judicial behavior is interdependent: Judges' actions are, in part, a function of their expectations about the actions of others. To say that a judge acts strategically is to say that she realizes that her success depends on the preferences of other relevant actors and the actions she expects them to take, not just on her own preferences and actions. On strategic accounts of judicial behavior, "other relevant actors" include the judges' colleagues (if they work on a collegial court) of course, but also their judicial superiors (if they serve on a non-apex court), elected officials, and the public – in other words, anyone in a position to help judges achieve their goals or stand in their way.

This component of the strategic account is in direct juxtaposition to most other approaches to judicial behavior. The attitudinal model and extreme legalism, for example, hold that judges always make choices that reflect their sincere preferences – whether to align decisions with their ideological commitments or to follow the law. Under the strategic account, whether judges behave sincerely or in a sophisticated fashion (that is, in a way that is not compatible with their most preferred position) depends on the preferences of the other relevant actors and the actions they are likely to take.

2.3 Institutions

Strategic accounts assume that judging takes place within a complex institutional framework. By institutions, we mean rules that structure the judges' interactions among themselves or with other relevant actors, and, ultimately, that may constrain them from acting on their sincere preferences. Institutions can be informal, such as norms and conventions. They can also be formal, such as "law" (broadly construed to include constitutional provisions, statutes, past judicial decisions, and the like) (Knight, 1992). So outlined, this approach to institutions highlights a key difference between legalism and strategic analysis. Extreme legalists argue that adherence to the law is a positive, not just normative, goal (i.e., judges derive pleasure from following previously decided cases) (Friedman, 2001), whereas strategic accounts tend to treat law as a formal institution that structures judicial decisions or that serves as a means to institutional or even personal ends. Examples include Knight and Epstein's (1996a) assertion that *stare decisis* ("to stand by things decided") helps judges to issue efficacious decisions; and Posner's (1993) claim that adhering to precedent increases opportunities for leisure by saving time, relative to deciding each case from first principles. Running along similar lines, Guerriero (2016) and Anderlini, Felli, and Riboni (2020) endogenize the extent of discretion that appellate judges can exploit under different legal traditions and show that a larger degree of judicial autonomy helps limit both the volatility of precedents and the inconsistency of rulings (see also Hanssen, 2004).

Whether formal or informal, institutions can be internal to the court – for example, the Supreme Court of Canada's institution that allows the chief justice to set the size and composition of panels (Alarie and Green, 2017) or the US Supreme Court's norm governing opinion assignment, which holds that the chief justice assigns the opinion of the court if he is in the majority (Lax and Rader, 2015). Institutions can also be external, governing relations between higher (or international) and lower (or domestic) courts (Cross and Tiller, 1998; Sweet and Brunell, 1998; Blanes i Vidal and Leaver, 2013, 2016; Dyevre, 2013; Masood and Lineberger, 2020), between courts and other governmental actors (Gely and Spiller, 1990; Eskridge, 1991a; Carrubba, Gabel, and Hankla, 2008; Larsson and Naurin, 2016; Arguelhes and Hartmann, 2017) and with the public (Knight and Epstein, 1996a; Friedman, 2009; Krehbiel, 2016). (All topics covered in Sections 4 and 5.)

Of course, the internal and external often work in concert, as made plain in research on rules governing the retention of judges. We already mentioned a study demonstrating that relatively short nonrenewable terms can cause judges to make strategic decisions designed to enhance their career prospects (Melcarne, 2017); the same holds for formal constitutional provisions forcing judges to face the electorate to retain their job (Huber and Gordon, 2004; Berdejó and Yuchtman, 2013; Canes-Wrone, Clark, and Kelly, 2014). Norms can play a similar role. Helmke (2002), for example, establishes that the Argentine constitution's assurance that judges "hold their office during good behavior" (the same as the US constitution) is little more than a parchment guarantee: "good behavior" does not mean life tenure as it is understood in the United States; it is instead a norm that has come to mean tenure for the life of the appointing regime. As Helmke writes: "[I]ncoming governments in Argentina routinely get rid of their predecessors' judges despite constitutional guarantees" (p. 292). Out of fear for their jobs or even their lives, Helmke theorized and empirically demonstrated that Argentine judges rationally anticipate the threat and begin "strategically defecting" by voting against the existing regime once it begins to lose power.

3 Conducting Strategic Analysis

With the basics of strategic analysis now fleshed out, we turn to the question of how scholars conduct the analysis. To be sure, debates ensue over the "best" approach but to us they are about as fruitful as debates over the "best" kinds of method and data – that is, not very (see Epstein, Šadl, and Weinshall, 2021). The fact of it is, at least four ways exist to "do" strategic analysis, none of which is superior to the others.

The first and perhaps most obvious is formal equilibrium analysis.[19] Although strategic analysis is not synonymous with formalization – indeed, various forms of strategic behavior can be fruitfully analyzed without formal work (Schelling, 1960; North, 1990) – that does not diminish the importance of formal analysis for many issues related to judicial behavior. If scholars hope to explain a particular line of decisions or a substantive body of law as the

---

[19] We adapt some of this discussion from Epstein and Knight (2000).

equilibrium outcome of the interdependent choices of the judges and other actors, they must demonstrate why the choices are in equilibrium, and a formal model is an essential feature of such a demonstration. For this reason game-theoretic analyses, in particular, are quite prevalent in the literature, whether used as a descriptive or analytic tool (see, generally, Snidal, 1986).

Incorporating the logic of strategic action into interpretive-historical research is a second approach to the analysis of interdependent behavior. Studies in this category differ in their particulars, but the overarching goal is to gain new insights into strategic problems confronting judicial actors. The problems could center on the judges' decisions in the context of cases – such as the classic showdown between President Thomas Jefferson and Chief Justice John Marshall in *Marbury* v. *Madison* (1803) (Clinton, 1994; Knight and Epstein, 1996b) – or even with regard to more personal choices – such as the decision to leave the bench (Squire, 1988; Vining, Smelcer, and Zorn, 2006).

A third approach is to use microeconomic theories to reason by analogy. This strategy is especially common in studies of the relationship between lower and higher courts, wherein scholars often develop an analogy between principal-agent theory and the judicial hierarchy. In common-law judicial systems, the correspondences work as follows (see, e.g., Songer, Segal, and Cameron, 1994).

economic marketplace → judicial system

principal → supreme court

agent → appellate court

utility maximizing economic actors → policy-maximizing judges

economic actors and judges both act strategically

With the analogy in hand, scholars draw inferences that become testable hypotheses – for example, if monitoring by a principal influences the behavior of the agent, then monitoring (reviewing) by a higher court should boost the responsiveness of the lower courts and constrain shirking (Songer, Segal, and Cameron, 1994; Westerland et al., 2010; Carrubba, Gabel, and Hankla, 2012).

Finally, many studies translate the strategic intuition into variables included in statistical models of judicial decisions. The outcomes of interest vary considerably – from deciding to hear a case (Black and Owens, 2012) to abstaining from a vote (Muro and Chehtman, 2020) to crafting majority opinions (Maltzman, Spriggs, and Wahlbeck, 2000). But the basic approach is the same: to determine statistically whether inputs designed to capture interdependent behavior explain outcomes.

Application of these four approaches remains widespread (reinforcing our earlier claim that none is superior), with all contributing to the strategic analysis of judicial behavior. Many contemporary studies, however, combine one or more of the approaches (Helmke, 2005; Vanberg, 2005). Pérez-Liñán and Arya's (2017) paper on strategic retirement supplies an example. After formally deriving hypotheses about the effect of partisan incentives on judicial retirements, the researchers assess them against data drawn from six presidential regimes.[20]

4 Strategic Analysis in Action I: Internal Accounts

The Pérez-Liñán and Arya study, as well as others we have mentioned, offers a glimpse into the value of strategic analysis. In what follows, we take a closer look at the ways strategic analysis provides insight into how internal judicial actors and actors external to courts affect the judges' choices. We begin with internal accounts and move in the next section to external accounts – although that distinction often blurs, as will quickly become apparent.

4.1 Judicial Colleagues (The "Collegial Court")

Internal accounts typically fall into one of two categories: judicial colleagues (the "collegial court") and judicial superiors (the "hierarchy of justice"). Then, within the colleagues' literature, two sets of choices have come under analysis: selecting cases and deciding cases. Because both have generated their fair share of studies, we emphasize especially interesting and important findings.

4.1.1 Selecting Cases

To deal with the piles of petitions (complaints) that come through their doors, most apex courts – whether common-law supreme courts or European-style constitutional courts – operate under rules that give them substantial discretion to select which cases they will hear and decide (Perry, 1991; Flemming, 2004; Fontana, 2011; Chowdhury, 2016; Alarie and Green, 2017).

In exercising discretion over their dockets, conventional wisdom has it that judges are quite strategic. In the US Supreme Court, strategic behavior takes the form of forward thinking: When deciding whether to hear a case, the justices take into account their odds of ultimately prevailing on the merits, given the preferences and likely actions of their colleagues (Perry, 1991; Caldeira, Wright and Zorn, 1999; Black and Owens, 2009). If a justice believes her preferred side will win down the road, she might cast an "aggressive grant" – a vote to hear a case even if she agrees with the lower court's decision – to give the ruling the weight of precedent. If she believes her side will lose she might cast a defensive denial – a vote against hearing a case even though she would like to reverse the decision below. A study of the Brazilian Supreme Court identifies a parallel

---

[20] Argentina, Brazil, Chile, Mexico, Panama, and the United States.

approach, in which individual justices, "unconstrained by the Court's internal rules of procedure," seek to delay or even indefinitely remove cases until the court's composition (or the political context) is more favorable toward their goals (Arguelhes and Hartmann, 2017).

For apex courts elsewhere, however, scant evidence exists that judges make these sorts of strategic calculation about their colleagues' likely behavior. A lack of internal vote data for scholars to mine may account for the void but more likely it reflects different institutions governing case selection and decision making, including the use of panels on many apex courts. Think about it this way: Because all nine US justices participate in all cases, it is not much of a stretch to believe they can predict how their colleagues will ultimately vote on the merits. Now consider the task on say, the Canadian Supreme Court. There, three of the nine justices sit on a gatekeeping panel, which decides whether the court should hear a case; if the panel answers in the affirmative, the chief justice creates another panel to hear and resolve the dispute. Under these rules, forward thinking would require the gatekeepers to anticipate (a) the chief justice's choice of the size and composition of the panel assigned to hear the case and (b) the votes of the justices selected by the chief. Obviously, it is much harder "to game the system" on the Canadian court; and data suggest that the justices don't bother (Alarie and Green, 2017).[21]

Considering the different internal institutions, many non-US studies of case selection focus less on forward thinking with regard to colleagues (and the policy goal) than on strategic calculations about external actors. In some accounts, the judges set their agenda with an eye toward avoiding cases that could create collisions with the regime or otherwise interfere with their ability to issue efficacious decisions, that is, to achieve institutional goals (Lavie, 2017). For example, after its confrontation with the government in 1993, the justices of the Russian Constitutional Court devoted fewer spots on their docket to the kinds of cases that got them in trouble (e.g., separation of powers and federalism) and far more to those that could enhance their popularity with the public (Epstein, Knight, and Shvetsova, 2002).

The Russian court is not alone. As Delaney (2016, 3) puts it, "avoidance is everywhere." The Israeli Supreme Court occasionally stays away from controversies by deciding not to decide (Reichman, 2013); and US justices use their power of docket control "to avoid entering some polarizing political debates," such as those over the constitutionality of particular wars (Fontana, 2011, 628). Then there's the study of the Italian Constitutional Court noted earlier

---

[21] A different strategic solution on some courts with rotating panels is to strategically select the panel instead of the cases, as detailed in the next section.

(Melcarne, 2017). The author finds that the justices attempt to enhance their post-court career prospects (a personal goal) by accepting high-profile cases – for example, those involving the participation of the prime minister because "the direct interest of the Executive in a case increases the relevance of such decision to the eyes of a rational judge willing to maximize her reputation."

4.1.2 Deciding Cases

The case-selection literature tells us that judges occasionally engage in strategic behavior to advance their personal, policy, or institutional goals. Such behavior continues when it comes to reaching decisions on disputes they have agreed to resolve.

Focusing on internal accounts (leaving the external for the next section), the literature is quite substantial, uncovering evidence of strategic behavior at almost all stages of the decision-making process. A few examples suffice to make the point.

Questioning Attorneys. Studies suggest that oral hearings involve not only the obvious – dialogues between the judges and lawyers – but also strategic interactions among the judges themselves; and that information communicated during those interactions can influence the judges' choices (Johnson, 2004; Epstein, Landes, and Posner, 2010; Black, Sorenson, and Johnson, 2013). The results from these studies fit quite compatibly with work by Iaryczower, Shi, and Shum (2018) showing that, under certain conditions, pre-vote deliberation can lead to better collective outcomes.

Composing Panels. The US Supreme Court always sits *en banc*, while the US Courts of Appeals (circuit courts) almost always decide cases in panels of three judges. Judges on peak courts outside the United States also usually sit in panels, but panel assignment is not necessarily random (as it supposedly is on the US circuits); and panel size is not formally set at three or at any other number for that matter. In place of the "no-discretion" rules operating in the USA, various institutions allow the court's leader to have a say over which and how many judges will sit on panels (Alarie and Green, 2017; Hanretty, 2020).

Some courts operate like the Canadian Court: The chief justice has nearly unfettered discretion to set panel composition and size (five, seven, or *en banc* at nine) (Alarie and Green, 2017). In the UK Supreme Court, the registrar composes the panels, but president of the court may override the registrar's decisions (Hanretty, 2020). On the discretion scale, chief justices in India and Australia are somewhere between Canada and the United Kingdom. Although they have power to assign panels, various rules constrain their choices. For example, on the Indian

Supreme Court, where some thirty justices serve, panels may not be smaller than two and must consist of at least five judges for important constitutional disputes (Alarie and Green, 2017). Even so, the rules leave ample room for court leaders to engage in strategic panel composition. And available evidence, culled from courts across the globe, suggests that they do just that, especially in cases of high salience (Haynie, 2002; Hausegger and Haynie, 2003; Sill and Haynie, 2010; Sommer, 2010; Alarie and Green, 2017; Givati and Rosenberg, 2020).

Why the power to compose panels is so valued is not hard to understand. The composers believe, plausibly so, that who sits on the panel affects how the dispute will be resolved. Sometimes the resolutions reflect the individual judges' tastes, but studies also shore up "panel," "collegial," or "peer" effects. The idea behind this line of research is that a case's outcome (or a judge's vote) would have been different had a single judge, and not a panel, decided the case (Kastellec, 2007). Often the focus is on the racial (Cox and Miles, 2008; Kastellec, 2013), gender (Boyd, Epstein, and Martin, 2010), or political/ideological (Cross and Tiller, 1998) makeup of the panel, although scholars have added other attributes to the mix, including the relative size of contributions to the panelists from organized interests (Iaryczower and Shum, 2012). The posited mechanisms vary too. Studies on race and gender, which find that even one woman or person of color on a panel can affect outcomes in relevant areas of the law (e.g., employment discrimination), tend to lean on informational explanations (that is, the "minority" judges possess information, experience, or expertise that is valuable to their colleagues). Research on political panel effects, in contrast, tends to turn on concerns about hierarchical superiors reversing the panel's decision – a subject to which we turn soon (in Section 4.2).

Assigning the Opinion of the Court. US chief justices do not compose panels but a related norm allows them to assign the opinion of the court when they are in the majority (Maltzman, Spriggs, and Wahlbeck, 2000; Lax and Cameron, 2007; Farhang, Kastellec, and Wawro, 2015; Lax and Rader, 2015). Not surprisingly, research on assignment has produced ample evidence of strategic behavior – for example, chief justices sometimes deliberately decline to cast a vote at a conference ("passing") when they are uncertain about whether they will be in the majority so that they can control opinion assignment (Epstein and Knight, 1998a; Johnson, Spriggs, and Wahlbeck, 2005). Then, when doling out assignments, strategic calculations also come in to play, such as assigning the opinion of the court to allies or to the justice most likely to defect from the majority (Rohde, 1972; Lax and Rader, 2015). Hanretty's (2020) results are similar for the UK Supreme Court: "UK judges who agreed more with the presiding judge [are] more likely to write a leading opinion."

Writing Opinions. A rather substantial literature applies strategic analysis to several aspects of opinion writing. One is the process of generating a majority opinion. On the US Supreme Court, once the majority opinion writer circulates a draft opinion, the other justices may attempt to bargain and negotiate with her. Strategic analyses have sought to delineate the circumstances under which justices will accept the opinion or write separately (Spriggs, Maltzman, and Wahlbeck, 1999; Lax and Cameron, 2007; Lax and Rader, 2015).

Second, and relatedly, is the extent to which judges engage in sophisticated opinion writing, compromising their own vision of the law to win over ambivalent colleagues or, at the least, snatch (some) victory from the jaws of defeat. There is evidence of this behavior on the US Supreme Court (Epstein and Knight, 1998a; Maltzman, Spriggs, and Wahlbeck, 2000), as well as among international court judges motivated to maximize decisions favoring particular states (Dothan, 2018).

Finally, an interesting literature considers how judges make strategic use of citations when writing their opinions. Frankenreiter (2017), for example, demonstrates that members of Court of Justice of the European Union (CJEU) "are more likely to cite judgments authored by judges appointed by Member State governments with similar preferences regarding European integration." Likewise Voeten (2010) finds that European Court of Human Rights (ECtHR) judges who favor a broad approach to the European Convention are more likely to cite decisions from other courts.

These opinion-writing studies tend to portray judges as policy-oriented, attempting to issue decisions that align the law with their political commitments. But strategic behavior with regard to colleagues does not always follow from policy motivations; personal concerns also may be at work. Epstein, Landes, and Posner (2011), for example, examine what they call "dissent aversion" on US circuit courts, wherein judges refrain from dissenting even if they disagree on ideological grounds with the majority opinion. The authors hypothesized, and found, that dissents impose costs on nondissenting judges (and therefore impose collegiality costs on the dissenter), while yielding minimal benefits to a dissenter in the form of prestige or recognition. A clever analysis of the Brazilian Supreme Court, too, finds evidence of dissent aversion tracing to nonideological considerations (de Mendonça Lopes, 2019). Taking advantage of the court's use of sequential voting, the study shows that justices who vote after the court's "pivotal" player are far less likely to dissent. Although it does not focus on dissents, Blanes I Vidal and Leaver's (2013, 80) is in much the same vein. The authors find that English appellate judges "randomly assigned to work with the authors of a given opinion are substantially more likely to cite their opinion as a persuasive authority than judges without such an interaction."

Institutional concerns may also figure in opinion writing. In addition to finding that ECtHR judges use citations to advance their policy goals, Voeten (2010, 549) demonstrates that the judges sometimes refrain from so doing because "they may feel constrained by potential state responses if judicial reasoning sets precedent and if compliance pressures are high." So too research on CJEU shows that when the court issues a decision in conflict with the position of EU member states, "the judges more strongly embed [it] in case law" (Larsson et al., 2017). (Because these are not the only studies highlighting the external-strategic aspects of opinion writing, we return to the topic in Section 5.2.2.)

4.2 Judicial Superiors (The "Hierarchy of Justice")

Much of the literature we have discussed pertains to relations between judges and their immediate colleagues. Another line of strategic work also focuses on the judiciary but moves beyond the judge's courtroom to the hierarchical structures in which many courts operate. In common-law systems, courts of last resort (e.g., the Norwegian, Israeli, and Japanese supreme courts) may have the opportunity to review decisions made by appellate courts; and appellate courts, the decisions of trial courts.

Review of this sort probably wouldn't matter too much if all judges at all levels agreed (i.e., if they all shared the same utility function). But because value conflicts are likely as pervasive in the judiciary as they are in most other organizations, the actors face challenges in meeting their goals: (1) lower court judges do not want to be reversed and (2) higher courts want to extract conformity from a subordinate court. (Hence the ubiquity of the principal-agent analogy, drawn earlier, even for research on civil-law systems.) Achieving these objectives requires both lower and higher courts to act strategically. Judicial inferiors must take into account the preferences and likely actions of their superiors, potentially altering their behavior to avoid reversal. Likewise, judicial superiors must develop mechanisms to ensure compliance.

On this much scholars tend to agree, although they differ on some of the particulars. Beginning with lower court judges, the questions of why they care about being reversed and how they attempt to avoid reversal are matters of some debate. The vast majority of US studies rest on policy motives to explain reversal aversion on the theory that when judges are reversed their (ideological) view of the law fails to carry the day (Kastellec, 2007; Randazzo, 2008; Boyd, 2015a). Studies elsewhere agree that judges dislike being reversed but offer more personal motivations – a difference that may trace to judicial selection and promotion procedures outside the USA, especially the influence of senior judges' recommendations. Recall that UK judges work to avoid reversals because they hurt the judges' reputation, decreasing the odds of promotion (Salzberger and Fenn, 1999); and, apparently, UK higher courts "are reluctant to reverse the judgments of [judges] with whom they are about to interact" (Blanes i Vidal and Leaver, 2016; see also Blanes i Vidal and Leaver, 2013). In Japan, which values "uniform and predictable legal standards," lower court judges who are out of step could find themselves moved to less prestigious locations (Tokyo is most desirable) or stuck in judgeships lacking administrative power (Ramseyer and Rasmusen, 2006).

Regardless of the driving force behind reversal aversion, scholars have observed strategic behavior consistent with it, although again the details vary from study to study. One line of literature, foreshadowed in our discussion of panel effects, follows from work by Cross and Tiller (1998), examining how judges attempt to avoid reversal by considering not only the preferences of fellow panel members but also the preferences and likely actions of their hierarchical superiors. The idea is that when a lower court appellate panel (in their study, a US circuit court panel) is ideologically homogeneous, the judges tend to reach more extreme decisions; in other words, homogeneity amplifies the effect of ideology. The panel can get away with this extreme behavior because, as Cross and Tiller explain, it lacks a "whistleblower" – a judge whose preferences differ from those of the majority and who will expose the majority's extremeness to the higher court (here, the US Supreme Court) via a dissent. Mixed panels, in contrast, will reach more moderate decisions because, by definition, a potential whistleblower is always present.[22] Put simply, the presence of whistleblowers can constrain their colleagues from behaving in accord with their sincere preferences (see also Kastellec, 2007, 2011; Beim and Kastellec, 2014).

Related to the "whistleblower" literature is a second set of studies that considers how lower courts treat higher court precedent when the lower courts believe that the contemporaneous higher court no longer supports the precedent. Broadly speaking, the results indicate that lower courts rationally anticipate and are quite sensitive to the shifting preferences of the higher court, suggesting that fear of reversal is more powerful than the urge to follow precedent (Westerland et al., 2010).

---

[22] Studies of single-judge trial courts reach a similar conclusion. They show that the judges strategically anticipate the likely reactions of the appellate court that could review their decisions, such that "liberal judges will reach more conservative decisions than they otherwise would as the probability of reversal by the appellate court increases, and likewise for conservative judges" (Randazzo, 2008; see also Boyd, 2015a).

Yet a third line of work focuses on how judges write opinions to insulate themselves from reversal. Some studies use simple metrics, hypothesizing, for example, that lower court judges facing ideologically diverse superiors will write longer, better justified decisions (Boyd, 2015b). Others draw on linguistic theory to explore the kinds of language (such as "hedging") that are less likely to provoke reversals (Hinkle et al., 2012). Regardless of the approach, the studies show that opinion-writing strategies can be effective in thwarting reversals when the upper and lower courts are politically distant.

Turning to hierarchically superior courts, how can they extract conformity from a subordinate court with different preferences? For those higher courts that may not hire, fire, promote, demote, financially reward, or penalize lower court judges, research has proposed various mechanisms for keeping lower courts honest. These include strategic auditing (Spitzer and Talley, 2000; Cameron, Segal, and Songer, 2000); running (implicit) tournaments among lower courts (McNollgast, 1995); writing clearer, more certain decisions (Corley and Wedeking, 2014); and, relying on whistleblowers to issue dissents (Lindquist, Haire, and Songer, 2007; Black and Owens, 2012).

5 Strategic Analysis in Action II: External Accounts

Work on internal judicial interactions continues, and will no doubt produce even more breakthroughs as the targets of inquiry expand beyond US courts. Nonetheless the bulk of modern-day strategic work worldwide has focused on relations between courts and external actors. This focus may reflect concerns among judges, lawyers, and scholars alike about threats posed by governments to courts in many societies (Bugaric and Ginsburg, 2016; Voeten, 2020). These days, politicians have not been reluctant to take to social media to deride court decisions or even threaten particular judges (Krewson, Lassen, and Owens, 2018; Okun, 2020). The rise of populism also has led to backlashes against both international and domestic courts (Voeten, 2020).

External strategic accounts speak to these concerns. They suggest that judges must render efficacious rulings – those that members of their society will respect and with which they will comply[23] – if they are to achieve their goals (Hall, 2014). In some external accounts, ideological or partisan motivations are featured, with judges acting strategically to ward off a legislative response that sets policy further from their most preferred point (Eskridge, 1991a, b; Epstein, Martin, and Knight, 2001; Harvey and Friedman, 2006). In other research more personal goals are at stake, including the judges' desire to keep their job, avoid targeted sanctions, and even ensure their safety (Knight and Epstein, 1996b; Helmke,

---

[23] There are some exceptions. See note 25.

2002, 2005; Helmke and Sanders, 2006). And in yet a third set of studies, judges are motivated to protect the independence and integrity of their institution against calls for "reform," whether proposals to add judges (court-packing), strip juris-diction, or eliminate judicial review, among many others (Rosenberg, 1992; Clark, 2011). Whatever the particular goal – from maximizing ideological pref-erences to warding off attacks – external accounts emphasize that achieving them requires judges to issue efficacious decisions, which, in turn, requires them to consider the preferences and likely actions of external actors who could override or otherwise thwart their rulings.

This is but an outline of external strategic accounts. Scholars have filled it in by exploring the particular methods available to judges desiring to render decisions that others will follow, and, ultimately, to establish their institution's legitimacy. In what follows we consider four sets of methods proposed and assessed in the literature: (1) anticipate the reactions of current external actors, (2) anticipate the reactions of incoming external actors, (3) time decisions, and (4) cultivate public opinion. Note that strategic analysts have yet to specify formally the circumstances under which one method might work better than others, although no doubt this is an important task for scholars to undertake.

5.1 Why the Need for Strategic Behavior?

Before turning to the methods for maximizing efficacy and legitimacy, we should address one possible objection to most external strategic accounts: namely, that they are unnecessary. This objection is grounded in one of three conceptions of courts – as reflections of the ruling regime, as unconstrained actors, and as super-strategists[24] – all of which suggest that inefficacious judicial decisions are none-vents, occurring rarely, if ever.

On the ruling regime conception, "the policy views dominant on the Court are never for long out of line with the policy views dominant among lawmaking majorities" and so conflicts between judges and elected actors are highly unlikely (Dahl, 1957). Put another way, the odds of issuing inefficacious deci-sions are quite small because political actors and judges share the same political preferences due to periodic turnover: Every few years, the ruling regime will have an opportunity to appoint new judges, and those new judges will make decisions in accord with their sincere political preferences, which happen to coincide with the views of those who appointed them. The second conception

---

[24] A fourth objection follows from "insurance theory," which holds that the relative competitive-ness of a country's party system determines whether its courts will act independently (Ramseyer, 1994) – with seemingly little role for courts to play in their own destiny. But this theory's assumptions are so numerous and stringent (see Stephenson, 2003; Vanberg, 2015) that few scholars have developed evidence to support its predictions.

treats European-style constitutional courts, in particular, as unconstrained actors (or even as chambers of government) with the power to "recast policy-making environments, to encourage certain legislative solutions while under-mining others, and to have the precise terms of their decisions written directly into legislative provisions" (Stone, 1995, 225). This conception seems to follow from a sequence of policymaking in which the government makes the first move by passing laws and the court has "last licks" to determine the laws' constitutionality, with its decisions final and formally binding (Ferejohn and Weingast, 1992). Hence, the court constrains elected actors but it need not worry about the preferences and likely actions of the government. On the third conception – judges as super-strategists – in equilibrium, no attacks on courts will ever occur because judges can prevent them by perfectly anticipating the preferences and likely actions of their would-be attackers (Eskridge, 1991a, b; Epstein and Knight, 1998a; Richman, Bergara, and Spiller, 2003).

A quick response to all three is that the real world provides evidence to the contrary, that the conceptions do not seem to explain the data we observe. If they did, only rarely would courts overturn laws passed by the contemporaneous regime (the ruling regime theory's prediction); or would elected actors (and the public) fail to comply with judicial decisions (the unconstrained actors' predic-tion); or would governments suspend their courts, threaten impeachment against particular judges, or take other steps to punish them or render their decisions inefficacious (super-strategists). But all these things happen, and they happen regularly in both advanced and evolving democracies (Clark, 2011; Bugaric and Ginsburg, 2016; Helmke, 2017).

Why? More pointedly, why don't the mechanisms in the three conceptions seem to work as expected? Because others provide detailed responses (Ferejohn, Rosenbluth, and Shipan, 2007; Epstein and Jacobi, 2010; Epstein and Knight, 2018), it is enough to note here that their assumptions are not often met. Take super-strategist accounts. The underlying mechanism is likely right – judges must be forward-thinking if they hope to issue efficacious decisions and build respect for their institution. But more often than not the assumption of perfect foresight is not satisfied. Mistakes happen owing to a lack of complete and perfect information about the relevant players' preferences, their likely actions, or both (Ferejohn, Rosenbluth, and Shipan, 2007; Larsson and Naurin, 2016).[25]

---

[25] Another problem is the possibility that some judges under some circumstances do not care all that much about the efficacy of their decisions because the failed decision will not be as bad as the alternatives (Helmke, 2017). When a society has the power to impeach its judges (or worse) and regularly uses it, that may be a bigger threat than, say, a government willing to override decisions, decrease the court's budget, or pack it with political hacks. Under these circumstances,

As for the ruling regime account: It assumes periodic turnover – such that the government has an opportunity to appoint new judges who will hold sway on the court. It turns out, however, that "moving the median" is very hard, as Krehbiel (2007) demonstrates for courts with life-tenured judges. Even mandatory retirement or term limits – rules in effect for most European constitutional court judges – do not guarantee a median aligned with the ruling regime (Epstein, Knight, and Shvetsova, 2002).

Finally, the unconstrained actor conception assumes that the court issues its decisions and that's that: all actors will comply. But as Vanberg (2005) points out, constitutional courts are "dependent on the cooperation of governing majorities ... to lend force to their decisions." This may be especially true in evolving democracies where courts have yet to establish their independence, legitimacy, and authority within the government. Because the courts are young (and sometimes operate in countries with a longheld suspicion of judges), they have yet to build reservoirs of support from which to draw when confronted with threats (Gibson, Caldeira, and Baird, 1998).

5.2 Anticipate the Reactions of Current External Actors

The upshot is this: In almost any society the preferences of the judges and the ruling regime/public will fail to align; value conflicts will emerge. How might courts respond? In what follows, we consider several approaches beginning here with the most prominent and well-rehearsed: anticipating the reactions of relevant external actors and responding accordingly even if that means engaging in sophisticated behavior (Eskridge, 1991a, b; Vanberg, 2005; Segal, Westerland, and Lindquist, 2011). Again, the central idea is that courts can work to ensure the integrity of their rulings by attending to the preferences and likely reactions of external actors in a position to respect or thwart them.

Of course, there is no guarantee that this strategy will always work for the reasons previously emphasized (e.g., lack of perfect information). But the literature suggests that judges can increase their chances of minimizing conflict and maximizing efficacy and legitimacy by undertaking one or more of the following approaches: interpret law dynamically, write vague opinions, and create rules designed to acquire information.[26]

---

judges will weigh the costs and benefits of reaching a decision they prefer over one the regime prefers (Ferejohn, Rosenbluth, and Shipan, 2007). Judges may well find themselves in situations in which they are at odds with the regime but where the reprisals are not very severe or enduring, tipping the balance towards benefits (Spiller and Tiller, 1996).

[26] This is not an exhaustive list. Another approach is to use internal institutions to make adjustments when efficacy is questionable. Hanretty (2020, 95), for example, demonstrates how the UK Supreme Court increases the size of panels to pressure the government to comply with its

5.2.1 Interpret Dynamically

Whether in the constitutional or statutory context, judges invoke various methods for interpreting text, to state the obvious. One such method, dynamic interpretation, is based on the premise that judges should read acts of government or constitutional provisions in line with the preferences and likely actions of the contemporaneous regime – not the desires, intent, or understanding of the framers (enacters) of the law or provision (Eskridge, 1991,a, b; Epstein, Knight, and Martin, 2001; Harvey and Friedman, 2006).[27]

When engaging in dynamic interpretation, it is possible that courts will find their preferences aligned with the relevant external actors (as ruling regime accounts predict), in which case they can act as they wish. Likewise, certain forms of political fragmentation may give judges more room to maneuver. Iaryczower, Spiller, and Tommasi (2002), for example, find that the Argentine Supreme Court tends to rule in favor of the government when the regime is unified but is often "defiant" when the regime is divided.

If the government is relatively united and the judges' preferences are distant from it, however, sophisticated behavior provides a plausible path – and one that judges often take. Well-developed data and case studies in the US context indicate that Supreme Court justices modify their interpretations of laws and constitutional provisions to consider possible reactions from Congress and the president (Richman, Bergara, and Spiller, 2003; Segal, Westerland, and Lindquist, 2011). So doing results in decisions that attempt to narrow the gap between the preferences of the judges and those of the other branches of government. The 2002 study by Iaryczower et al. suggests the same for Argentine justices, as do similar analyses of courts in Russia (Epstein, Knight, and Shvetsova, 2002), Germany (Vanberg, 2005), and Israel (Sommer, 2010), among others.

5.2.2 Write Vague Opinions

Dynamic interpretation may receive the lion's share of attention but it is not the only method available to judges facing potential opposition to their rulings.

---

decisions: "If the court wishes to attract extra attention to the case because it fears that the government will drag its feet in complying, it should therefore sit in a larger panel."

Also worth reiterating is that the same techniques are relevant not only for maximizing institutional and policy goals, but also for advancing personal goals; for example, when judges with promotion expectations anticipate the public's (and their representatives') preference for harsher sentencing (Epstein, Landes, and Posner, 2013) or vote consistently with the president's preferences (Black and Owens, 2016).

[27] Recall that lower courts in the United States engage in this form of behavior vis-à-vis the Supreme Court. Rather than interpreting a precedent in accord with the will of the enacting court, they rationally anticipate the preferences and likely response of the current court (Westerland et al., 2010).

Earlier, we noted studies demonstrating how courts use citations to enhance the odds of compliance with their decisions (Voeten, 2010; Larsson et al., 2017). A related strategy, suggested by Staton and Vanberg (2008), centers on the clarity (or lack thereof) of opinions. The researchers assume that that the costs to implementers of deviating from a clear court decision are higher than the costs of deviating from a vague decision because noncompliance is easier to detect. So if a court faces friendly implementers, it may be better off writing clear opinions; clarity increases pressure for and thus the likelihood of compliance. But when the probability of opposition from implementers is high, clarity could be costly to the judges. If policymakers are determined to defy even a crystal-clear decision, they highlight the relative lack of judicial power. To soften anticipated resistance, courts may be purposefully vague.[28]

Staton and Vanberg (2008) provide several interesting examples of the strategic use of vagueness, including the Warren Court's 1955 decision in *Brown* v. *Board of Education II* and the German Constitutional Court's rulings in two important taxation cases. In both, the justices had the same reason for leaving ambiguous "the precise actions that would be consistent with the decision": concerns about compliance and, ultimately, legitimacy. And now more systematic evidence supports Staton and Vanberg's ideas. Black et al. (2016), for example, show that US justices strategically craft language in their opinions, adjusting the level of clarity to correspond to their assessment of the likelihood of noncompliance by external actors, including federal agencies and the states. Sternberg (2018) adds more nuance to the Staton-Vanberg model, demonstrating that courts' use of vagueness is related to their level of public support. Whereas the French Conseil Constitutionel, a court with low support, uses vagueness "as a defensive mechanism to hide noncompliance from public view" – a finding that comports with Staton-Vanberg's model – the German Constitutional Court, which enjoys higher public support, uses vague language "to strategically pressure the legislature."

5.2.3 Uncover Preferences and Likely Actions

Knowing when to write clear versus vague decisions requires judges to learn about the preferences and likely actions of those able to block achievement of their goals. To that end, we should, and do, see courts develop information-acquiring rules and procedures (Spriggs and Wahlbeck, 1997; Epstein and Knight, 1998b; Johnson, 2004; Collins, 2008).

---

[28] There is a parallel result in the literature on the judicial hierarchy: Corley and Wedeking's (2014) finding that lower courts are more likely to follow high court decisions written at higher degrees of certainty.

Exemplary in the United States are rules governing the participation of *amici curiae* ("friends-of-the-court," although, in US courts, almost always "friends" of one side or the other). Likely out of the belief that government *amicus* briefs can advance its project of learning about the response of a key implementer (or potential thwarter) the court maintains a rather lax rule, allowing state and federal officials to file without the parties' consent. All other would-be *amici*, mostly nongovernmental organizations, must obtain written consent from both parties or file a motion with the court if consent is withheld. Nonetheless, by granting almost all such motions, the justices have signaled to the parties not to deny consent in the first place (O'Connor and Epstein, 1983). The same holds for the Canadian Supreme Court, where the justices "grant almost all interest group applications for leave to intervene" (Brodie, 2002, 36). Leniency in this context seems sensible. Although groups do not convey the government's preferences, they can play a role in generating support for (or opposition to) the court's decision.

The analysis by Carrubba et al. of the Court of Justice of the European Union (CJEU) also shows the potency of information-acquiring rules. In cases pending before the court, EU institutions and member state governments can file briefs (called "observations"), which help the CJEU assess the "balance of member-state preferences regarding the legal issue" (Carrubba, Gabel, and Hankla, 2008, 440). The more observations for one side, the higher the chances of that side winning. Which, again, makes good sense: If the member states favor one side and the court rules the other way, the states could form a coalition to override the decision, thereby rendering it ineffective (see also Larsson and Naurin, 2016).

These results and, more relevant here, the very fact that the CJEU allows government observations, are not surprising. Courts must place a premium on lawyering as a form of information transmission if they are to anticipate the reaction of relevant external actors. Moreover, to the extent that encouraging a diversity of inputs will likely lead to better decisions (Posner, 1996), using rules to learn about preferences has benefits beyond the strategic context of decision making.

5.3 Anticipate the Reactions of Incoming External Actors

The approaches just outlined pertain to judicial behavior toward the current regime. Helmke's studies (2002, 2005) on Argentina, recall, suggest another possibility: When judges fear impeachment or worse, they will concern themselves less with contemporaneous actors than with the incoming regime. An analysis of Korea, Taiwan, Thailand, and Pakistan concurs. In disputes over "whether prominent political figures could retain or take office," courts in these countries tend to support the electorate's preferences. As a result, the judges play a role in facilitating transitions to democracy but only after the "transition is secured" (Ginsburg, 2013, 46).

What of countries where democratic institutions are less fragile and the courts less fearful of retaliatory tactics on the part of the incoming regime? Anticipation of the desires of the new leaders still may be a useful approach for courts hoping to ensure their place in the new order. Gillman's (2001) book on *Bush* v. *Gore* (2000) makes the nice point that a majority of justices on the US Supreme Court ruled the way they did because they had political cover: They knew the incoming regime would support their selection of Bush over Gore.

More generally, a great deal of empirical work (although, regrettably, mostly US-centered) suggests that judges do seem to follow the election returns or at least the "mood" of the public (McGuire and Stimson, 2004; Giles Blackstone, and Vining, 2008; Casillas, Enns, and Wohlfarth, 2011). But the mechanism is unclear. Here (and in the sections to follow), we posit that judges bend to the will of the people because they and their court require public support to remain an efficacious branch of government (Friedman, 2009). The existing studies could be read to support this view, but they are equally consistent with another mechanism: that "the people" include judges. On this account, judges are not directly affected by public opinion but rather respond to the same events or forces that affect the opinion of other members of the public. To quote US Justice Benjamin N. Cardozo (1921, 168), "[t]he great tides and currents which engulf the rest of men do not turn aside in their course and pass the judges by" (for more on this debate, see Epstein and Martin, 2010; Casillas, Enns, and Wohlfarth, 2011). Then again, the two mechanisms need not be mutually exclusive. Hofnung and Weinshall-Margel's (2010) study, remember, demonstrates that Israeli justices use latent methods, unseen by the public, to propose settlements in security-force cases following terror attacks, but apply more publicly open methods during times of peace.

5.4 Time Decisions

Deciding when to propose settlements, as well as docket monitoring via careful case selection, can be quite effective in staving off attacks and controversy. But these are not only way courts evade; strategic adjustments in the timing of their decisions are another. Fontana (2011, 629) reports that "many of the world's most successful constitutional review courts waited several years – until the politics of the situation had cooled off some – before deciding major cases related to the responses by the political branches to the events of September 11, 2001." The German Constitutional Court, the House of Lords, and the US Supreme Court issued no major decisions until 2004 or 2005; the High Court of Australia waited until 2007.

Likewise, Delaney (2016) documents the South African Constitutional Court's occasional practice of delaying a suspension of invalidity to allow the legislature to respond to its decision (see also Lau, 2016). The Canadian courts follow suit – and in high-profile cases at that. Consider that when the US Supreme Court invalidated all existing bans on same-sex marriage, its decision had immediate effect: Gays could marry in every US state. Not so in South Africa and Canada, where the courts "explicitly deferred the effect of decisions to recognize a right to same sex equality, giving provincial and national legislatures twelve to twenty-four months to respond to their decisions" (Dixon and Issacharoff, 2016, 685). These delays might be focused on concerns about "the practical costs of immediately effective judicial decisions." But some suspensions "look strategic" – designed to promote institutional legitimacy (Delaney 2016, 49).

Evidence on strategic timing also comes from large *n* research. We already mentioned Argueles and Hartmann's (2017) study establishing that Brazilian Supreme Court justices delay hearing a case or announcing a decision until the justices believe there is a more favorable political climate (or a court more inclined to rule their way). Epstein, Landes, and Posner (2015, 1022) show that the US Supreme Court issues its most important, controversial, and divisive decisions at the end of its term. A possible explanation is that: "[T]he justices delay certain decisions for public-relations reasons. The close proximity of decisions in the most important cases may tend to diffuse media coverage of and other commentary regarding any particular case, and thus spare the justices unwanted criticism."

5.5 Cultivate Public Opinion

The point of avoidance doctrines is to avoid disputes that may harm the judiciary in both the short and long terms. To the extent that it calls on courts to go on the offensive, the final approach – cultivating public opinion – is something of the reverse: If judges can develop deep support among voters, they can increase the costs of noncompliance by elected officials, thereby offsetting the benefits of court bashing (Vanberg, 2005). Or, as Magalhães and Garoupa (2020, 1743) aptly put it: "Ultimately, courts that lack the public's trust and support may be more vulnerable to attempts by political actors to undermine judicial independence, checks and balances, and the rule of law."

Seen in this way, "public support provides a shield for judicial independence" (Vanberg, 2015, 177). When judges generate public confidence in their institution and their rulings, they advance their cause with the ruling regime by lengthening the elected actors' "tolerance intervals" – intervals around the actors' ideal points such that they would be unwilling to challenge a court decision placed within that interval (Epstein, Knight, and Shvetsova, 2002).

What methods are available to courts wishing to increase the costs of attacks via the public? The extant literature proposes a number of possibilities, including issuing decisions that are consistent with public opinion. Whether that approach generalizes beyond the United States (and, perhaps, Israel), however, remains unclear owing to a paucity of research. Fortunately, other approaches have been assessed more globally, with two moving to the fore: when judges "go public" and when they attempt to develop popular rights.[29]

5.5.1 Go Public

Staton's (2010, 7) important book, *Judicial Power and Strategic Communication in Mexico*, documents the Mexican Supreme Court's "coordinated and aggressive" public relations campaign. The Court's goal was to generate conditions as favorable as possible to the exercise of its power. As Staton writes: "[C]ommunication strategies are broadly designed to advance the transparency of the conflicts constitutional courts resolve and to promote a deep societal belief in the judicial legitimacy, conditions that promote judicial power."

The Mexican Supreme Court is not alone. According to Staton, judges serving on constitutional courts throughout the world now go public, attempting to engage the citizenry through various channels. Publicizing their decisions is

---

[29] Four other approaches worth mentioning are, first, efforts by judges to convince the public that they "are not merely legislators in robes but are constrained by professional codes of conduct that transcend their narrow policy preferences." They can accomplish this by, for example, justifying "their decisions with respect to the constitutional text" – which elected politicians typically don't do (Vanberg, 2015, 179).

The second occurs when judges incorporate public sentiment into the court's jurisprudence. For example, to determine whether a particular punishment the government wants to impose is "cruel and unusual" and so forbidden by the 8th Amendment of the US Constitution, the Supreme Court has said: "The words of the [8th] Amendment are not precise, and ... their scope is not static. The Amendment must draw its meaning from the evolving standards of decency that mark the progress of a maturing society" (*Trop* v. *Dulles*, 1958). To assess whether a punishment comports with "evolving standards" of decency, judges can and do look at public opinion polls (see, e.g., *Atkins* v. *Virginia*, 2002).

Third, experimental evidence from the United States and Norway shows that dissenting opinions can (contrary to conventional wisdom) actually boost support for courts because they amount to consolation prizes for people who disagreed with the decision: even losers get representation (Salamone, 2018; Bentsen, 2019).

Finally, Magalhães and Garoupa (2020, 1743) report that judges can increase citizens' trust through their courts' performance in resolving cases efficiently.

commonplace: Nearly 90 percent of the courts Staton studied make them available on the Internet; many also issue press releases announcing (select) decisions. And it is now hard to identify a court that doesn't maintain a website housing information about its procedures, cases, and even bios of its members.

These are indirect, passive forms of communication but, as Staton also shows, more direct contact is not uncommon – especially efforts by judges "to use the media to underline key jurisprudential points," such as giving interviews to clarify rulings, delivering lectures to justify opinions, and even publishing letters to urge compliance with controversial decisions. Frishman (2017) adds to the list, providing examples of apex courts worldwide producing movies and books, opening court museums and gift shops, and even creating advertisements and dedicated television channels.[30] Frishman likens these methods to the techniques used by public relations firms to promote various causes, and argues that they are pivotal for the courts' ability to gain public support.

Although some of these methods are new, "going public" is not. In the wake of the US Supreme Court's controversial decision in *McCulloch* v. *Maryland* (1819) Chief Justice John Marshall wrote several articles responding to his critics under the nom de plume "A Friend of the Union." Then there was Chief Justice Earl Warren's insistence that his court issue a short, nonrhetorical, nontechnical opinion in the landmark case of *Brown* v. *Board of Education* (1954).

Whether deploying old or more innovative methods, the objective is to enhance public support for the court, thereby making it more costly for the regime to undermine it. The success of these methods, however, is another matter – and one ripe for study. An analysis of the websites of courts in three judicial systems (Italian, Dutch, and New York State), for example, shows that enhancing legitimacy requires sites to meet certain established criteria (such as, supervision and access) (Velicogna and Ng, 2006). Needless to write, not all do.

5.5.2 Develop (Popular) Rights

If contemporary papers are any indication, an equally common method of appealing to the public is to protect or entrench rights that have broad appeal. Mate (2013) attributes judicial empowerment in India to the Supreme Court's development of a "jurisprudential regime" of public interest litigation (see also Rosenberg, Krishnaswamy, and Bail, 2019). Under this regime, the Court

---

[30] See, for example, TVJUSTICA (www.tvjustica.jus.br/index/conheca), a channel operated by the Secretariat of Social Communication of the Supreme Court of Brazil.

"expansively interpreted fundamental rights," articulated a new "nonarbitrariness standard," and relaxed standing requirements. It seems that the South African Court hewed to a similar approach: "The Court ... gave confidence to white elites that it would protect property and economic rights, guaranteeing some degree of continuity. At the same time, it gave confidence to black majorities that the democratization process was going to mean a real change for them" (Klug, 2013). Similarly, research on Singapore paints a portrait of judges working not so much to protect individual dignity but rather to achieve a collective goal: economic development and the "strengthening of state institutions" (Silverstein, 2008).

Whatever the approach, the objective, once again, is the same: to increase the costs of attacking the court and thus to broaden the tolerance intervals of elected actors. Ferejohn and Pasquino (2003, 250) put it this way: "Perhaps the popularity of constitutional courts has grown with their demonstrated effectiveness in protecting rights, [leaving] the governing coalition with less political room for undermining court autonomy."

6 Moving Forward

No doubt, strategic accounts have gone some distance toward illuminating judicial behavior. Happily for us researchers, however, many opportunities remain for forward movement. We have flagged several throughout but here we are more specific, identifying four directions: theoretical, comparative, empirical, and normative.

Let's start with the theoretical. As noted at the outset, strategic accounts assume that the judge "is a rational maximizer of his ends in life, his satisfactions ... his 'self-interest'" (Posner, 2011, 3). This strikes us as a reasonable assumption, or at least one that gets us pretty far in understanding the choices judges make. But it will not get us all the way there. It is just too late in the day to question the "thinking-fast" approach to judging (see Table 1), which amounts to decades' worth of studies showing that in many situations, people rely heavily on heuristics ("rules of thumb"), intuitions, and the like to make fast decisions without much effort. These responses aren't invariably wrong or even unhelpful (Wistrich, Rachlinski, and Guthrie, 2015); in fact, scholars of behavioral economics, psychology, and administration invoke the term "rational heuristics" to suggest that supposed "cognitive shortcuts" sometimes form the "basis of value-creating strategies that can be more effective than information-intensive, cognitively demanding approaches" (Bingham and Eisenhardt, 2011; see also Gigerenzer, 2016). Nonetheless, in many circumstances fast thinking, unchecked by deliberative assessments, can lead to mistakes and biased decisions (Kahneman, 2011;

Thaler, 2015), enticing people "away from making optimal decisions in terms of utility maximization" (Das and Teng, 1999).

Although judges seem to believe that they can "suppress or convert" their biases, prejudices, sympathies, and the like into rational decisions (Wistrich, Rachlinski, and Guthrie, 2015), this is not so. Experiments conducted on thousands of judges demonstrate that they respond more favorably to litigants they like or with whom they sympathize (Wistrich, Rachlinski, and Guthrie, 2015), fall prey to hindsight bias when assessing probable cause (Rachlinski, Guthrie, and Wistrich, 2011), harbor implicit bias toward Black defendants (Rachlinski et al., 2009), use anchoring and other simplifying heuristics when making numerical estimates (Sonnemans and van Dijk, 2012), "find" evidence to confirm their beliefs (Rachlinski, Guthrie, and Wistrich, 2013), and favor insiders and disfavor outgroups (Wistrich, Rachlinski, and Guthrie, 2015). Judges, it turns out, are human too (Guthrie, Rachlinski and Wistrich, 2001, 2007; see also Simon and Scurich, 2013; Spamann and Klohn, 2016).

To the extent that judges are influenced by their emotions, intuitions, and biases it complicates their ability to make strategically rational decisions. And thus it complicates our efforts to explain their behavior. There is no getting around the fact that these very human features can distort purely strategic decision making. The interesting yet-to-be answered research questions relate to how much and in what ways insights from the experiments alter what we would expect to see if we assume judges act rationally. A potential avenue for relevant research would be to compare the predictions of strategic analysis with data on actual judicial decisions, while accounting for the possibility of thinking-fast judging (for possible approaches, see Shayo and Zussman, 2011; Epstein, Parker, and Segal, 2018; Segal, Sood, and Woodson, 2018). This would give us a better sense of the extent to which nonrational factors influence the judges' choices.

Truth be told, though, such studies are not easy to pull off because of the problem of behavioral equivalence: here, when rational and thinking-fast accounts predict the same behavior. Posner and de Figueiredo's study (2005) on the International Court of Justice (ICJ) provides an example. After demonstrating that ICJ judges tend to vote in favor of their home country, the authors offer an explanation that fits compatibility with strategic rationality (p. 608):

> Economically, judges may be motivated by material incentives. Judges who defy the wills of their government by holding against it may be penalized. The government may refuse to support them for reappointment and also refuse to give them any other desirable government position after the expiration of their term.

But another mechanism is equally plausible: ICJ judges side with their own country not because they are rationally advancing an economic or any other interest but because of an emotional response. Posner and de Figueiredo recognize as much when they offer this alternative explanation for their finding (p. 608):

> Psychologically, if judges identify with their countries, they may find it difficult to maintain impartiality. International Court of Justice judges are not only nationals who would normally have strong emotional ties with their country; they also have spent their careers in national service as diplomats, legal advisors, administrators, and politicians. Even with the best intentions, they may have trouble seeing the dispute from the perspective of any country but that of their native land.

Epstein and Posner (2016) confront the same problem in a study finding that US justices are loyal to the president who appointed them. To be sure, loyalty could be understood as a form of strategic behavior under which judges sacrifice policy goals to advance more personal interests, such as reciprocity and the preservation of bonds.[31] Then again, as Epstein and Posner write (2016, 408): "[L]oyalty can also be the result of indoctrination and education. People may learn to be loyal to political authorities; they may *instinctively* be loyal to family members; they may develop loyalty to friends and colleagues with whom they overcome common obstacles."

We could go on; the problem of behavioral equivalence is that rampant. At the same time, however, with clever designs and data scholars can and, more to the point, *must* overcome it if we are to develop more comprehensive explanations of judicial behavior.

Accounting for nonrational factors is the theoretical approach we commend. The second avenue, on comparative research, is better paved, but there is still some distance to go. Certainly, the field of judicial behavior, once owned by US-based political scientists, has grown into a worldwide enterprise as this Element showcases. Throughout we have mentioned studies spanning from Argentina (Helmke 2002, 2005), Brazil (Arguelhes and Hartmann, 2017), and Chile (Carroll and Tiede 2012) up to Mexico (Staton, 2010) and Canada (Brodie, 2002; Flemming, 2004); and from Japan (Ramseyer and Rasmusen, 2006) across the globe to India (Mate 2013; Chowdhury, 2016), Israel (Weinshall-Margel, 2011; Givati, 2020), and most of Europe (Garoupa et al., 2013; Melcarne, 2017; Hanretty, 2020), down to South Africa (Sill and Haynie, 2010) and Australia (Weiden, 2011) and extending to international and transnational courts (Voeten 2008; Dothan, 2018).

---

[31] Loyalty could also be seen as rational in another way: as just half a quid pro quo. In economic models of cooperation, one agent's loyalty to another depends on the other's loyalty to the first.

And yet, in spite of the increasing attention to comparative analysis of strategic judicial behavior, a large asymmetry is still evident between the number of studies on US judges and those working elsewhere. Not to put too fine a point on it, vast swaths of substantive work on US judges have received little attention in many corners of the world. Whether courts follow the public's mood is an especially noticeable gap if only because research findings may well transport worldwide (although perhaps the lack of systematic public opinion data stands in the way). But there are many other unexplored areas, including the aforementioned "loyalty effect," which may be even more consequential outside the USA, especially in societies where strong links exist among legal, political, and economic elites. On the flipside, more studies of Asian, African, Latin American, and Australian courts could prove illuminating for research on judging in the USA. To provide one example: Debate ensues in the USA over whether to swap life tenure for a single nonrenewable term. Research on the career paths of the many judges who serve for set terms – where they come from, where they go after serving, and, crucially, whether their decisions are related to their subsequent career choices – would no doubt inform US debates, in addition to having value in their own right.

New comparative work could come in two (major) varieties: analyses of courts/judges serving in one country (in a single era or over time) or cross-national studies of many courts/judges. Most of the studies covered here fall into the former category,[32] and by all means that work should continue. At the same time, the acceleration of research analyzing judges and courts across societies would be a welcome development. By comparing judges with different competencies, audiences, and institutions, scholars can tackle a long list of interesting research questions. These include some we have already mentioned (such as career paths and public opinion), as well as those focusing on how the "rules of the game" – whether over panel formation, judicial appointment, methods of review – structure strategic interactions (see, generally, North, 1990).

Although cross-national studies designed to answer these questions are likely to be high-reward projects, they also pose high risks and many challenges. Studying judicial behavior across societies requires in-depth knowledge of the different judicial systems. Comparisons that are merely technical or formalistic may not be especially satisfying, as the compared concepts are often contested, difficult to measure, and may have different meanings in different places.

---

[32] Exceptions include Weiden, 2011; Garoupa and Ginsburg, 2015; Alarie and Green, 2017; Brouard and Hönnige, 2017; Pérez-Liñán and Arya, 2017; Weinshall, Sommer, and Ritov, 2017; Voeten 2020.

Which brings us to the third recommendation: the creation of high-quality data infrastructure for the analysis of judicial behavior within and across countries. This recommendation may be obvious to scholars working in the field; they regularly bemoan the fact that data have not kept pace with increased interest in judging worldwide. The problem seems to be that scholars (mostly)[33] continue to work in isolation building datasets precisely tailored to their theoretical framing, definitions, and hypotheses and centered on particular courts, countries, or regions. This "one-off" approach has its benefits, of course. But it also has substantial costs, ultimately impeding the march toward knowledge, innovation, and invention. These costs include the massive duplication of effort, inefficiencies, and dated (if not downright unreliable) measures and data (see Weinshall and Epstein, 2020).

Forward movement in the strategic analysis of judicial behavior calls for the development of modern, reliable, and sustainable large-scale public databases. Case-level data are crucial, and, ideally, would include not only relatively easy-to-collect inputs and outputs (e.g., the date of decision, the parties to the suit, the judges' identities and votes, the winner) but also information extracted from the texts judges produce. Some progress has been made along these lines (e.g., Hinkle et al., 2012; Boyd, 2015b; Black et al., 2016). But mostly we have taken the equivalent of methodological baby steps (Rice and Zorn, 2020). In thinking about judges' opinions as text as data, imagine extracting, for example, more nuanced information about the judges' preferences, along with other dimensions of interest to strategic analysts. And we need not be limited to judicial opinions. Analysis of oral argument audios and transcripts to assess, for example, the role of rational and nonrational factors is quite feasible (Vunikili et al., 2018; Dietrich, Enos, and Sen, 2019). Likewise, a wealth of information could be extracted from briefs, just as scholars have done with the language in financial texts (e.g., corporate reports) (Lewis and Young, 2019).

However vital case-/opinion-based datasets may be, they are not the only tools that would advance the strategic analysis of judicial behavior. Equally vital is infrastructure focused on institutional features of courts, including downright basic information (e.g., the salary of apex court judges, their caseload, the way they get and keep their job, even the name of their court). Because

---

[33] Happily, there are a growing number of exceptions. For instance, the Argentine Supreme Court Project (at the Universidad Torcuato di Tella); the European Court of Human Rights Database (https://depts.washington.edu/echrdb/); the German Federal Courts Dataset (Hamann, 2019); the Israeli Supreme Court Database (Weinshall and Epstein, 2020); and the Norwegian Supreme Court Database (Grendstad, Shaffer, and Waltenburg, 2015). And many others are in the works (on the Inter-American Court of Human Rights, the Court of Justice of the European Union, the Costa Rican Supreme Court, the German Federal Constitutional Court, and the Swedish Supreme Court).

no high-quality compilation of the relevant particulars exists, we are constantly looking them up and assembling them ourselves. And we can't believe we are alone in this; institutional "facts" are, recall, relevant to almost accounts of judicial behavior.

Building these sorts of dataset for courts worldwide may sound like the impossible dream but it's not.[34] By automating data collection to the extent possible (Grimmer and King, 2011; Grimmer and Stewart, 2013), filling in the gaps with crowd-sourced coding by experts and nonexperts alike (Benoit et al., 2016; Carlson and Montgomery, 2017) and resisting irrational data exuberance (Weinshall and Epstein, 2020), they are entirely possible enterprises.

Creating new infrastructure, as well as the theoretical and comparative directions we have proposed, are designed to appeal to the many social scientists who study judicial behavior. Our last proposal, however, may fall out their comfort zone because it entails marrying strategic studies and traditional legal analysis to enrich normative debates over the role that the judiciary should play in democratic systems *and* the role of academic research in advancing the judiciary's legitimacy.

At first blush, this doesn't seem like a marriage made in heaven. Whereas traditional doctrinal analysis explores the content of law from a legal-internal point of view to find normatively justifiable rules, judicial behavior research usually adopts a positive perspective, striving to describe and explain the judges' choices and their consequences. And while law scholars often explore legal structure, argument, and interpretation by applying doctrinal legal analysis, judicial behavior research mostly draws on scientific methodologies to achieve its goals. Last, but certainly not least, the central component of strategic analysis – that judges are strategic actors who attend to "extraneous" factors when deciding legal disputes – is one that many mainstream legal scholars find troubling. They worry that studies showing the importance of political and personal preferences could undermine the courts' legitimacy (see Gibson and Caldeira, 2011).

For these reasons, literature integrating (traditional) legal and strategic approaches is relatively scarce.[35] Nonetheless, we believe that the two have much to learn from each other – and much to contribute to the study of judging.

---

[34] Two examples of related projects are the Comparative Constitutions Project (https://comparati veconstitutionsproject.org), a useful source for formal constitutional rules; and Varieties of Democracy (www.v-dem.net/en/), which contains data on expert judgments about features of legal systems worldwide.

[35] Exceptions include Peretti (2001), arguing that politically motivated constitutional decision making is not only inevitable, but also legitimate and desirable; and Stewart and Stuhmcke (2020), advocating the creation of ethical guidelines to enable, yet constrain, "judicial analytics" (the use of data to monitor, understand, and predict judicial behavior).

Consider judicial review, a topic of perennial concern to scholars of law and legal institutions. On the one side, legal academics might question rules that allow courts to invalidate laws (i.e., to act in a countermajoritarian fashion) if judges are little more than strategic "politicans." On the other side, strategic analysts argue that only by acting strategically can judges establish and maintain the legitimacy of the courts. Surely it is possible for the two sides to work together to find some balance, perhaps in the form of institutions designed to minimize "bad" strategic behavior and maximize the "good."

This is but one example of the ways that traditional legal and strategic analysts can inform one another's work (for others, see Epstein, Šadl, and Weinshall, 2021). More generally, combining skill sets, paying greater heed to the literature on thinking-fast judging, drawing cross-national comparisons, and developing new data infrastructure present real opportunities for social scientists and legal academics alike. Seizing them and, of course, developing new directions along the way, will help ensure that the best days for the strategic analysis of judicial behavior are yet to come.

References

Alarie, Benjamin and Andrew J. Green. 2017. *Commitment and Cooperation on High Courts*. New York: Oxford University Press.

Anderlini, Luca, Leonardo Felli, and Alessandro Riboni. 2020. "Legal Efficiency and Consistency." *European Economic Review* 121: Article 103323.

Arguelhes, Diego Werneck and Ivar A. Hartmann. 2017. "Timing Control without Docket Control: How Individual Justices Shape the Brazilian Supreme Court's Agenda." *Journal of Law and Courts* 5(1): 105–40.

Barber, Michael and Jeremy C. Pope. 2019. "Does Party Trump Ideology? Disentangling Party and Ideology in America." *American Political Science Review* 13(1): 38–54.

Baum, Larry. 1997. *The Puzzle of Judicial Behavior*. Ann Arbor, MI: University of Michigan Press.

Baum, Larry. 2006. *Judges and Their Audiences: A Perspective on Judicial Behavior*. Princeton, NJ: Princeton University Press.

Baum, Lawrence. 2017. *Ideology in the Supreme Court*. Princeton, NJ: Princeton University Press.

Becker, Theodore L. 1970. *Comparative Judicial Politics: The Political Functioning of Courts*. Chicago, IL: Rand McNally.

Beim, Deborah and Jonathan P. Kastellec. 2014. "The Interplay of Ideological Diversity, Dissents, and Discretionary Review in the Judicial Hierarchy: Evidence from Death Penalty Cases." *Journal of Politics* 76(4): 1074–88.

Benoit, Kenneth, Drew Conwy, Benjamin E. Lauderdale, and Michael Laver. 2016. "Crowd-Sourced Text Analysis: Reproducible and Agile Production of Political Data." *American Political Science Review* 110(2): 278–95.

Bentsen, Henrik Litleré. 2019. "Dissent, Legitimacy, and Public Support for Court Decisions: Evidence from a Survey-Based Experiment." *Law & Society Review* 53(2): 588–610.

Berdejó, Carlos and Noam M. Yuchtman. 2013. "Crime, Punishment, and Politics: An Analysis of Political Cycles in Criminal Sentencing." *Review of Economics and Statistics* 95(3): 741–56.

Bingham, Christopher B. and Kathleen M. Eisenhardt. 2011. "Rational Heuristics: The 'Simple Rules' that Strategists Learn from Process Experience." *Strategic Management Journal* 32(13): 1437–64.

Black, Ryan C. and Ryan J. Owens. 2009. "Agenda Setting in the Supreme Court: The Collision of Policy and Jurisprudence." *Journal of Politics* 71(3): 1062–75.

Black, Ryan C. and Ryan J. Owens. 2012. "Consider the Source (and the Message): Supreme Court Justices and Strategic Audits of Lower Court Decisions." *Political Research Quarterly* 65(2): 385–95.

Black, Ryan C. and Ryan J. Owens. 2016. "Courting the President: How Circuit Court Judges Alter Their Behavior for Promotion to the Supreme Court." *American Journal of Political Science* 60(1): 30–43.

Black, Ryan C., Ryan J. Owens, Justin Wedeking, and Patrick C. Wohlfarth. 2016. *U.S. Supreme Court Opinions and their Audiences*. New York: Cambridge University Press.

Black, Ryan C., Maron W. Sorenson, and Timothy R. Johnson. 2013. "Towards an Actor- Based Measure of Supreme Court Case Salience: Information-Seeking and Engagement During Oral Arguments." *Political Research Quarterly* 66(4): 803–17.

Blanes i Vidal, Jordi and Clare Leaver. 2013. "Social Interactions and the Content of Legal Opinions." *Journal of Law, Economics, and Organization* 29(1): 78–114.

Blanes i Vidal, Jordi and Clare Leaver. 2016. "Bias in Open Peer-Review: Evidence from the English Superior Courts." *Journal of Law, Economics, and Organization* 31(3): 431–71.

Bonica, Adam and Maya Sen. 2021. "Estimating Judicial Ideology." *Journal of Economic Perspectives* 35(1): 97–118.

Boyd, Christina L. 2015a. "The Hierarchical Influence of Courts of Appeals on District Courts." *Journal of Legal Studies* 44(1): 113.

Boyd, Christina L. 2015b. "Opinion Writing in the Federal District Courts." *Justice System Journal* 36(3): 254–73.

Boyd, Christina L., Lee Epstein, and Andrew D. Martin. 2010. "Untangling the Causal Effect of Sex on Judging." *American Journal of Political Science* 54(2): 389–411.

Boyd, Christina L. and Jacqueline Sievert. 2013. "Unaccountable Justice? The Decision Making of Magistrate Judges in the Federal District Courts." *Justice System Journal* 34(3): 249–73.

Brodie, Ian. 2002. *Friends of the Court: The Privileging of Interest Group Litigants in Canada*. Albany, NY: SUNY Press.

Brouard, Sylvain and Christoph Hönnige. 2017. "Constitutional Courts as Veto Players: Lessons from the United States, France and Germany." *European Journal of Political Research* 56(3): 529–52.

Bugaric, Bojan and Tom Ginsburg. 2016. "The Assault on Postcommunist Courts." *Journal of Democracy* 27(3): 69–82.

Caldeira, Gregory A., John R. Wright, and Christopher J. W. Zorn. 1999. "Sophisticated Voting and Gate-Keeping in the Supreme Court." *Journal of Law, Economics, and Organization* 15(3): 549–72.

Cameron, Charles M. 1993. "Decision-Making and Positive Political Theory (Or, Using Game Theory to Study Judicial Politics)." Paper presented at the Wallis Institute of Political Economy, Rochester, NY.

Cameron, Charles M., Jeffrey A. Segal, and Donald R. Songer. 2000. "Strategic Auditing in a Political Hierarchy: An Informational Model of the Supreme Courts Certiorari Decisions." *American Political Science Review* 94(1): 101–16.

Canes-Wrone, Brandice, Tom S. Clark, and Jason P. Kelly. 2014. "Judicial Selection and Death Penalty Decisions." *American Political Science Review* 108(1): 23–9.

Cardozo, Benjamin. 1921. *The Nature of the Judicial Process*. New Haven, CT: Yale University Press.

Carlson, David and Jacob Montgomery. 2017. "A Pairwise Comparison Framework for Fast, Flexible, and Reliable Human Coding of Political Texts." *American Political Science Review* 111(4): 835–43.

Carroll, Royce and Lydia Tiede. 2012. "Ideological Voting on Chile's Constitutional Tribunal: Dissent Coalitions in the Adjudication of Rights." *Journal of Human Rights* 11(1): 85–105.

Carrubba, Clifford J., Matthew J. Gabel, and Charles Hankla. 2008. "Judicial Behavior under Political Constraints: Evidence from the European Court of Justice." *American Political Science Review* 102(4): 435–52.

Carrubba, Clifford J., Matthew Gabel, and Charles Hankla. 2012. "Understanding the Role of the European Court of Justice in European Integration." *American Political Science Review* 106(1): 214–23.

Casillas, Christopher J., Peter K. Enns, and Patrick C. Wohlfarth. 2011. "How Public Opinion Constrains the U.S. Supreme Court." *American Journal of Political Science* 55(1): 74–88.

Chowdhury, Rishad Ahmed. 2016. "Missing the Wood for the Trees: A Critical Exploration of the Supreme Court of India's Chronic Struggle with its Docket." University of Chicago, JSD dissertation.

Clark, Tom S. 2011. *The Limits of Judicial Independence*. New York: Cambridge University Press.

Clark, Tom S., Benjamin G. Engst, and Jeffrey K. Staton. 2018. "Estimating the Effect of Leisure on Judicial Performance." *Journal of Legal Studies* 47(2): 349–90.

Clinton, Robert Lowry. 1994. "Game Theory, Legal History, and the Origins of Judicial Review." *American Journal of Political Science* 38(2): 285–302.

Collins, Paul M. 2008. *Friends of the Supreme Court: Interest Groups and Judicial Decision Making*. New York: Oxford University Press.

Cooter, Robert D. 1983. "The Objectives of Private and Public Judges." *Public Choice* 41(1): 107–32.

Corley, Pamela C. and Justin Wedeking. 2014. "The (Dis)Advantage of Certainty: The Importance of Certainty in Language." *Law & Society Review* 48(1): 35–62.

Coroado, Susana, Nuno Garoupa, and Pedro C. Magalhães. 2017. "Judicial Behavior under Austerity: An Empirical Analysis of Behavioral Changes in the Portuguese Constitutional Court, 2002–2016." *Journal of Law and Courts* 5(2): 289–311.

Cox, Adam B. and Thomas J. Miles. 2008. "Judging the Voting Rights Act." *Columbia Law Review* 108(1): 1–54.

Cross, Frank B. and Emerson H. Tiller. 1998. "Judicial Partisanship and Obedience to Legal Doctrine: Whistleblowing on the Federal Courts of Appeals." *Yale Law Journal* 107(7): 2155–75.

Dahl, Robert A. 1957. "Decision-Making in a Democracy: The Supreme Court as a National Policymaker." *Journal of Public Law* 6(Fall): 279–95.

Dalla, Lucia Pellegrina, Laarni Escresa, and Nuno Garoupa. 2014. "Measuring Judicial Ideal Points in New Democracies: The Case of the Philippines." *Asian Journal of Law and Society* 125(1): 125–64.

Das, T. K. and Bing-Sheng Teng. 1999. "Cognitive Biases and Strategic Decision Processes: An Integrative Perspective." *Journal of Management Studies* 36(6): 757–78.

de Figueiredo, Miguel F. P., Alexandra D. Lahav, and Peter Siegelman. 2019. "The Six-Month List and the Unintended Consequences of Judicial Accountability." *Cornell Law Review* 105: 363–456.

de Mendonça Lopes, Felipe. 2019. "Dissent Aversion and Sequential Voting in the Brazilian Supreme Court." *Journal of Empirical Legal Studies* 16(4): 933–54.

Delaney, Erin F. 2016. "Analyzing Avoidance: Judicial Strategy in Comparative Perspective." *Duke Law Journal* 66(1): 1–68.

Dietrich, Bryce J., Ryan D. Enos, and Maya Sen. 2019. "Emotional Arousal Predicts Voting on the U.S. Supreme Court." *Political Analysis* 27(2): 237–43.

Dixon, Rosalind and Samuel Issacharoff. 2016. "Living to Fight Another Day: Judicial Deferral in Defense of Democracy." *Wisconsin Law Review* 2016(4): 683–732.

Dothan, Shai. 2015. *Reputation and Judicial Tactics: A Theory of National and International Courts*. Cambridge: Cambridge University Press.

Dothan, Shai. 2018. "The Motivations of Individual Judges and How They Act as a Group." *German Law Journal* 19(7): 2165–88.

Drahozal, Christopher R. 1998. "Judicial Incentives and the Appeals Process." *SMU Law Review* 51(3): 469–503.

Dyevre, Arthur. 2010. "Unifying the Field of Comparative Judicial Politics: Towards a General Theory of Judicial Behavior." *European Political Science Review* 2(2): 297–327.

Dyevre, Arthur. 2013. "Filtered Constitutional Review and the Reconfiguration of Judicial Politics." *American Journal of Comparative Law* 61(4): 729–55.

Eisenberg, Theodore, Talia Fisher, and Issi Rosen-Zvi. 2012. "Does the Judge Matter? Exploiting Random Assignment on a Court of Last Resort to Assess Judge and Case Selection Effects." *Journal of Empirical Legal* Studies 9(2): 246–90.

Engel, Christoph and Lilia Zhurakhovska. 2017. "You are in Charge: Experimentally Testing the Motivating Power of Holding a Judicial Office." *Journal of Legal Studies* 46(1): 1–50.

Epstein, Lee and Tonja Jacobi. 2010. "The Strategic Analysis of Judicial Decisions." *Annual Review of Law and Social Science* 6: 341–58.

Epstein, Lee and Jack Knight. 1998a. *The Choices Justices Make*. Washington, DC: CQ Press.

Epstein, Lee and Jack Knight. 1998b. Mapping Out the Strategic Terrain: The Informational Role of Amici Curiae. In *Supreme Court Decision-Making*, eds. Cornell Clayton and Howard Gillman. Chicago, IL: University of Chicago Press.

Epstein, Lee and Jack Knight. 2000. "Toward a Strategic Revolution in Judicial Politics: A Look Back, A Look Ahead." *Political Research Quarterly* 53(3): 625–61.

Epstein, Lee and Jack Knight. 2013. "Reconsidering Judicial Preferences." *Annual Review of Political Science* 16: 11–31.

Epstein, Lee and Jack Knight. 2018. Efficacious Judging on Apex Courts. In *Comparative Judicial Review*, eds. Erin F. Delaney and Rosalind Dixon. Cheltenham: Edward Elgar.

Epstein, Lee, Jack Knight, and Andrew Martin. 2001. "The Supreme Court as a *Strategic* National Policy Maker." *Emory Law Journal* 50(2): 583–611.

Epstein, Lee, Jack Knight, and Olga Shvetsova. 2002. "The Role of Constitutional Courts in the Establishment and Maintenance of Democratic Systems of Government." *Law and Society Review* 35(1): 117–64.

Epstein, Lee, William M. Landes, and Richard A. Posner. 2010. "Inferring the Winning Party in the Supreme Court from the Pattern of Questioning at Oral Argument." *Journal of Legal Studies* 39(2): 433–67.

Epstein, Lee, William M. Landes, and Richard A. Posner. 2011. "Why (and When) Judges Dissent." *Journal of Legal Analysis* 3(1): 101–37.

Epstein, Lee, William M. Landes, and Richard A. Posner. 2013. *The Behavior of Federal Judges*. Cambridge, MA: Harvard University Press.

Epstein, Lee, William M. Landes, and Richard A. Posner. 2015. "The Best for Last: The Timing of U.S. Supreme Court Decisions." *Duke Law Journal* 64(6): 991–1022.

Epstein, Lee and Andrew D. Martin. 2010. "Does Public Opinion Influence the Supreme Court? Possibly Yes (But We're Not Sure Why)." *University of Pennsylvania Journal of Constitutional Law* 13(2): 263–82.

Epstein, Lee, Andrew D. Martin, Kevin Quinn, and Jeffrey A. Segal. 2012. Ideology and the Study of Judicial Behavior. In *Ideology and the Law*, ed. Jon Hanson. Oxford: Oxford University Press.

Epstein, Lee, Christopher M. Parker, and Jeffrey A. Segal. 2018. "Do Justices Defend the Speech They Hate? An Analysis of In-Group Bias on the U.S. Supreme Court." *Journal of Law and Courts* 6(2): 237–61.

Epstein, Lee and Eric Posner. 2016. "Supreme Court Justices' Loyalty to the President." *Journal of Legal Studies* 45(2): 401–36.

Epstein, Lee, Urkša Šadl, and Keren Weinshall. 2021. "The Role of Comparative Law in the Analysis of Judicial Behavior." *American Journal of Comparative Law*, forthcoming.

Eren, Ozkan and Naci Mocan. 2018. "Emotional Judges and Unlucky Juveniles." *American Economic Journal: Applied Economics* 10(3): 171–205.

Eskridge, William N., Jr., 1991a. "Overriding Supreme Court Statutory Interpretation Decisions." *Yale Law Journal* 101(2): 331–417.

Eskridge, William N., Jr., 1991b. "Reneging on History?: Playing the Court/Congress/President Civil Rights Game." *California Law Review* 79(3): 613–84.

Farhang, Sean, Jonathan P. Kastellec, and Greg Wawro. 2015. "The Politics of Opinion Assignment and Authorship on the U.S. Court of Appeals: Evidence from Sexual Harassment Cases." *Journal of Legal Studies* 44: S59–S85.

Ferejohn, John and Pasquale Pasquino. 2003. Rule of Law and Rule of Democracy. In *Democracy and the Rule of Law*, eds. José María Maravall and Adam Przeworski. Cambridge: Cambridge University Press.

Ferejohn, John, Francis Rosenbluth, and Charles Shipan. 2007. Comparative Judicial Politics. In *The Oxford Handbook of Comparative Politics*, eds. Carles Boix and Susan Stokes. Oxford: Oxford University Press.

Ferejohn, John and Barry Weingast. 1992. "A Positive Theory of Statutory Interpretation." *International Review of Law and Economics* 12(June): 263–79.

Fettig, Shawn C. and Sara C. Benesh. 2016. Be Careful With My Court: Legitimacy, Public Opinion, and the Chief Justices. In *The Chief Justice: Appointment and Influence*, eds. Artemus Ward and David Danelski. Ann Arbor, MI: University of Michigan Press.

Flemming, Roy B. 2004. *Tournament of Appeals: Granting Judicial Review in Canada*. Vancouver, BC: UBC Press.

Fontana, David. 2011. Docket Control and the Success of Constitutional Courts. In *Comparative Constitutional Law*, eds. Tom Ginsburg and Rosalind Dixon. Cheltenham: Edward Elgar Publishing.

Frankenreiter, Jens. 2017. "The Politics of Citations at the ECJ – Policy Preferences of E.U. Member State Governments and the Citation Behavior of Judges at the European Court of Justice." *Journal of Empirical Legal Studies* 14(4): 813–57.

Friedman, Barry. 2001. "Taking Law Seriously." *Perspectives on Politics* 4(2): 261–71.

Friedman, Barry. 2009. *The Will of the People*. New York: Farrar, Straus, & Giroux.

Frishman, Olga. 2017. "Court-Audience Relationships in the 21st Century." *Mississippi Law Journal* 86(2): 213–72.

Garoupa, Nuno and Tom Ginsburg. 2015. *Judicial Reputation: A Comparative Theory*. Chicago, IL: University of Chicago Press.

Garoupa, Nuno, Fernando Gomez-Pomar, and Veronica Grembi. 2013. "Judging under Political Pressure: An Empirical Analysis of Constitutional Review Voting in the Spanish Constitutional Court." *Journal of Law, Economics, and Organization* 29(3): 513–34.

Gely, Rafael and Pablo T. Spiller. 1990. "A Rational Choice Theory of Supreme Court Decision Making with Applications to the State Farm and Grove City Cases." *Journal of Law, Economics, and Organization* 6(2): 263–300.

George, Tracey E. and Lee Epstein. 1992. "On the Nature of Supreme Court Decision Making." *American Political Science Review* 86(2): 323–37.

Gibson, James L. and Gregory A. Caldeira. 2011. "Has Legal Realism Damaged the Legitimacy of the U.S. Supreme Court?" *Law & Society Review* 45(1): 195–219.

Gibson, James L., Gregory A. Caldeira, and Vanessa A. Baird. 1998. "On the Legitimacy of High Courts." *American Political Science Review* 92(2): 343–58.

Gigerenzer, Gerd. 2016. Towards a Rational Theory of Heuristics. In *Minds, Models and Milieu*, eds. Roger Frantz and Leslie Marsh. London: Palgrave Macmillan.

Giles, Micheal W., Bethany Blackstone, and Richard L. Vining. 2008. "The Supreme Court in American Democracy: Unraveling the Linkages Between

Public Opinion and Judicial Decision Making." *Journal of Politics* 70(2): 293–306.

Gillman, Howard. 2001. *The Votes that Counted*. Chicago, IL: University of Chicago Press.

Ginsburg, Tom. 2013. The Politics of Courts in Democratization. In *Consequential Courts*, eds. Diana Kapiszewski, Gordon Silverstein, and Robert A. Kagan. Cambridge: Cambridge University Press.

Givati, Yehonatan and Israel Rosenberg. 2020. "How Would Judges Compose Judicial Panels? Theory and Evidence from the Supreme Court of Israel." *Journal of Empirical Legal Studies* 17(2): 317–41.

Grendstad, Gunnar, William R. Shaffer, and Eric Waltenburg. 2015. *Policy Making in an Independent Judiciary: The Norwegian Supreme Court*. Colchester: ECPR Press.

Grimmer, Justin and Gary King. 2011. "General Purpose Computer-Assisted Clustering and Conceptualization." *Proceedings of the National Academy of Sciences* 108(7): 2643–50.

Grimmer, Justin and Brandon M. Stewart. 2013. "Text as Data: The Promise and Pitfalls of Automatic Content Analysis Methods for Political Texts." *Political Analysis* 21(3): 267–97.

Guerriero, Carmine. 2016. "Endogenous Legal Traditions and Economic Outcomes." *Journal of Comparative Economics* 44(2): 416–33.

Guthrie, Chris, Jeffrey J. Rachlinski, and Andrew J. Wistrich. 2001. "Inside the Judicial Mind." *Cornell Law Review* 86(4): 777–830.

Haire, Susan B. and Laura P. Moyer. 2015. *Diversity Matters: Judicial Policymaking on the U.S. Courts of Appeals*. Charlottesville, VA: University of Virginia Press.

Hall, Matthew E. K. 2014. "The Semiconstrained Court: Public Opinion, The Separation of Powers, and the US Supreme Court's Fear of Nonimplementation." *American Journal of Political Science* 58(2): 352–66.

Hamann, Hanjo. 2019. "The German Federal Courts Dataset 1950–2019: From Paper Archives to Linked Open Data." *Journal of Empirical Legal Studies* 16(3): 671–88.

Hamilton, Alexander. 1788. "Federalist Paper #78," available at https://avalon .law.yale.edu/18th_century/fed78.asp.

Hanretty, Chris. 2012. "Dissent in Iberia: The Ideal Points of Justices on the Spanish and Portuguese Constitutional Tribunals." *European Journal of Political Research* 51(5): 671–92.

Hanretty, Chris. 2020. *A Court of Specialists: Judicial Behaviour in the UK Supreme Court*. Oxford: Oxford University Press.

Hanssen, F. Andrew. 2004. "Is There a Politically Optimal Level of Judicial Independence?" *American Economic Review* 94(3): 712–29.

Harvey, Anna and Barry Friedman. 2006. "Pulling Punches: Congressional Constraints on the Supreme Court's Constitutional Rulings, 1987–2000." *Legislative Studies Quarterly* 31(4): 533–62.

Hausegger, Lori and Stacia Haynie. 2003. "Judicial Decisionmaking and the Use of Panels in the Canadian Supreme Court and the South African Appellate Division." *Law & Society Review* 37(3): 635–57.

Haynie, Stacia. 2002. "Judicial Decision-Making and the Use of Panels in the South African Appellate Division." *Politikon: South African Journal of Political Studies* 29(2): 147–61.

Helmke, Gretchen. 2002. "The Logic of Strategic Defection: Court-Executive Relations in Argentina Under Dictatorship and Democracy." *American Political Science Review* 96(2): 291–303.

Helmke, Gretchen. 2005. *Courts Under Constraints: Judges, Generals, and Presidents in Argentina*. Cambridge: Cambridge University Press.

Helmke, Gretchen. 2017. *Institutions on the Edge: The Origins and Consequences of Inter-Branch Crises in Latin America*. Cambridge: Cambridge University Press.

Helmke, Gretchen and Mitchell S. Sanders. 2006. "Modeling Motivations: A Method for Inferring Judicial Goals from Behavior." *Journal of Politics* 68(4): 867–78.

Hettinger, Virginia A., Stefanie A. Lindquist, and Wendy L. Martinek. 2006. *Judging on a Collegial Court: Influences on Federal Appellate Decision Making*. Charlottesville, VA: University of Virginia Press.

Hinkle, Rachael K., Andrew D. Martin, Jonathan D. Shaub, and Emerson H. Tiller. 2012. "A Positive Theory and Empirical Analysis of Strategic Word Choice in District Court Opinions." *Journal of Legal Analysis* 4(2): 407–44.

Hofnung, Menachem and Keren Weinshall Margel. 2010. "Judicial Setbacks, Material Gains: Terror Litigation at the Israeli High Court of Justice." *Journal of Empirical Legal Studies* 7(4): 664–92.

Hönnige, Christoph. 2009. "The Electoral Connection: How the Pivotal Judge Affects Oppositional Success at European Constitutional Courts." *West European Politics* 32(5): 963–84.

Huber, Gregory A. and Sanford C. Gordon. 2004. "Accountability and Coercion: Is Justice Blind when It Runs for Office?" *American Journal of Political Science* 48(2): 247–63.

Iaryczower, Matias, Xiaoxia Shi, and Matthew Shum. 2018. "Can Words Get in the Way: The Effect of Deliberation in Collective Decision Making." *Journal of Political Economy* 126(2): 688–734.

Iaryczower, Matias and Matthew Shum. 2012. "Money in Judicial Politics: Individual Contributions and Collective Decisions," available at https://ssrn.com/abstract=1998895.

Iaryczower, Matias, Pablo T. Spiller, and Mariano Tommasi. 2002. "Judicial Independence in Unstable Environments, Argentina 1935–1998." *American Journal of Political Science* 46(4): 699–715.

Johnson, Timothy. 2004. *Oral Arguments and Decision Making on the United States Supreme Court*. Albany, NY: SUNY Press.

Johnson, Timothy R., James F. Spriggs, and Paul J. Wahlbeck. 2005. "Passing and Strategic Voting on the U.S. Supreme Court." *Law & Society Review* 39(2): 349–77.

Kahneman, Daniel. 2011. *Thinking, Fast and Slow*. New York: Farrar, Straus, & Giroux.

Kantorowicz, Jaroslaw and Nuno Garoupa. 2016. "An Empirical Analysis of Constitutional Review Voting in the Polish Constitutional Tribunal, 2003–2014." *Constitutional Political Economy* 27: 66–92.

Kastellec, Jonathan P. 2007. "Panel Composition and Judicial Compliance on the U.S. Courts of Appeals." *Journal of Law, Economics, and Organization* 23(2): 421–41.

Kastellec, Jonathan P. 2011. "Hierarchical and Collegial Politics on the U.S. Courts of Appeals." *Journal of Politics* 73(2): 345–61.

Kastellec, Jonathan P. 2013. "Racial Diversity and Judicial Influence on Appellate Courts." *American Journal of Political Science* 57(1): 167–83.

Katz, Daniel M. 2006. "Institutional Rules, Strategic Behavior, and the Legacy of Chief Justice William Rehnquist: Setting the Record Straight on *Dickerson v. U.S.*" *Journal of Law and Politics* 22(4): 303–39.

Klein, David E. and Robert J. Hume. 2003. "Fear of Reversal as an Explanation of Lower Court Compliance." *Law & Society Review* 37(3): 579–606.

Klug, Heinz. 2013. Constitutional Authority and Judicial Pragmatism: Politics and Law in the Evolution of South Africa's Constitutional Court. In *Consequential Courts*, eds. Diana Kapiszewski, Gordon Silverstein, and Robert A. Kagan. Cambridge: Cambridge University Press.

Knight, Jack. 1992. *Institutions and Social Conflict*. Cambridge: Cambridge University Press.

Knight, Jack and Lee Epstein. 1996a. "The Norm of *Stare Decisis*." *American Journal of Political Science* 40(4): 1018–35.

Knight, Jack and Lee Epstein. 1996b. "On the Struggle for Judicial Supremacy." *Law and Society Review* 30(1): 87–130.

Krehbiel, Jay N. 2016. "The Politics of Judicial Procedures: The Role of Public Oral Hearings in the German Constitutional Court." *American Journal of Political Science* 60(4): 990–1005.

Krehbiel, Keith. 2007. "Supreme Court Appointments as a Move-the-Median Game." *American Journal of Political Science* 51(2): 231–40.

Krewson, Chris, David Lassen, and Ryan J. Owens. 2018. "Twitter and the Supreme Court: An Examination of Congressional Tweets about the Supreme Court." *Justice System Journal* 39(4): 322–30.

Larsson, Olof and Daniel Naurin. 2016. "Judicial Independence and Political Uncertainty: How the Risk of Override Affects the Court of Justice of the EU." *International Organization* 70(2): 377–408.

Larsson, Olof, Daniel Naurin, Mattias Derlén, and Johan Lindholm. 2017. "Speaking Law to Power: The Strategic Use of Precedent of the Court of Justice of the European Union." *Comparative Political Studies* 50(7): 879–907.

Lau, Holning. 2016. "Comparative Perspectives on Strategic Remedial Delays." *Tulane Law Review* 91(2): 259–323.

Lavie, Shay. 2017. "Discretionary Review and Undesired Cases." *European Journal of Law and Economics* 44(2): 265–85.

Lax, Jeffrey R. and Charles M. Cameron. 2007. "Bargaining and Opinion Assignment on the U.S. Supreme Court." *Journal of Law, Economics, and Organization* 23(2): 276–302.

Lax, Jeffrey R. and Kelly Rader. 2015. "Bargaining Power on the Supreme Court: Evidence from Opinion Assignment and Vote Switching." *Journal of Politics* 77(3): 635–47.

Lewis, Craig and Steven Young. 2019. "Fad or Future? Automated Analysis of Financial Text and Its Implications for Corporate Reporting." *Accounting and Business Research* 49(5): 587–615.

Li, Siyu. 2020. "A Separation-of-Powers Model of U.S. Chief Justice Opinion Assignment." *Justice System Journal* 41(1): 3–21.

Lindquist, Stefanie A., Susan B. Haire, and Donald R. Songer. 2007. "Supreme Court Auditing of the U.S. Courts of Appeals: An Organizational Perspective." *Journal of Public Administration Research and Theory* 17(4): 607–24.

Magalhães, Pedro C. and Nuno Garoupa. 2020. "Judicial Performance and Trust in Legal Systems: Findings from a Decade of Surveys in over 20 European Countries." *Social Science Quarterly* 101(5): 1743–60.

Maltzman, Forrest, James F. Spriggs, and Paul J. Wahlbeck. 2000. *Crafting Law on the Supreme Court: The Collegial Game*. New York: Cambridge University Press.

Masood, Ali S. and Monica E. Lineberger. 2020. "United Kingdom, United Courts? Hierarchical Interactions and Attention to Precedent in the British Judiciary." *Political Research Quarterly* 73(3): 714–26.

Mate, Manoj. 2013. Public Interest Litigation and the Transformation of the Supreme Court of India. In *Consequential Courts*, eds. Diana Kapiszewski, Gordon Silverstein, and Robert A. Kagan. Cambridge: Cambridge University Press.

McGuire, Kevin T. and James A. Stimson. 2004. "The Least Dangerous Branch Revisited: New Evidence on Supreme Court Responsiveness to Public Preferences." *Journal of Politics* 66(4): 1018–35.

McNollgast. 1995. "Politics and Courts: A Positive Theory of Judicial Doctrine and the Rule of Law." *Southern California Law Review* 68(6): 1631–83.

Melcarne, Alessandro. 2017. "Careerism and Judicial Behavior." *European Journal of Law and Economics* 44(2): 241–64.

Miceli, Thomas and Metin Cosgel. 1994. "Reputation and Judicial Decision-Making." *Journal of Economic Behavior and Organization* 23(1): 31–51.

Muro, Sergio and Alejandro Chehtman. 2020. "Law or Strategic Calculus? Abstention in the Argentine Supreme Court." *International Review of Law and Economics* 62: Article 105889.

Murphy, Walter F. 1964. *Elements of Judicial Strategy*. Chicago, IL: University of Chicago Press.

Narayan, Paresh Kumar and Russell Smyth. 2007. "What Explains Dissent on the High Court of Australia? An Empirical Assessment Using a Cointegration and Error Correction Approach." *Journal of Empirical Legal Studies* 4(2): 401–25.

North, Douglass C. 1990. *Institutions, Institutional Change, and Economic Performance*. Cambridge, MA: Cambridge University Press.

O'Connor, Karen and Lee Epstein. 1983. "Court Rules and Workload: A Case Study of Rules Governing Amicus Curiae Participation." *Justice System Journal* 8(1): 35–45.

Okun, Eli. 2020. "Trump Calls for Sotomayor, Ginsburg to Recuse Themselves from Cases Dealing with his Administration." Politico, February 25.

Ordeshook, Peter C. 1992. *A Political Theory Primer*. New York: Routledge.

Pérez-Liñán, Aníbal and Ignacio Arana Araya. 2017. "Strategic Retirement in Comparative Perspective: Supreme Court Justices in Presidential Regimes." *Journal of Law and Courts* 5(2): 173–97.

Peretti, Terry J. 2001. *In Defense of a Political Court*. Princeton, NJ: Princeton University Press.

Perry, H. W. 1991. *Deciding to Decide: Agenda Setting in the United States Supreme Court*. Cambridge, MA: Harvard University Press.

Posner, Eric A. and Miguel F. P. de Figueiredo. 2005. "Is the International Court of Justice Biased?" *Journal of Legal Studies* 34(2): 599–630.

Posner, Richard A. 1993. "What Do Judges and Justices Maximize? (The Same Thing Everybody Else Does)." *Supreme Court Economic Review* 3: 1–41.

Posner, Richard A. 1996. *The Problems of Jurisprudence.* Cambridge, MA: Harvard University Press.

Posner, Richard A. 2008. *How Judges Think.* Cambridge, MA: Harvard University Press.

Posner, Richard A. 2011. *Economic Analysis of Law.* New York: Aspen.

Pritchett, C. Herman. 1961. *Congress versus the Supreme Court.* Minneapolis, MN: University of Minnesota Press.

Rachlinski, Jeffrey J., Chris Guthrie, and Andrew J. Wistrich. 2011. "Probable Cause, Probability, and Hindsight." *Journal of Empirical Legal Studies* 8(1): 72–98.

Rachlinski, Jeffrey J., Chris Guthrie, and Andrew J. Wistrich. 2013. "Consilience in the Courtroom: Do Apologies Affect Adjudication?" *Cornell Law Review* 98(5): 1189–1244.

Rachlinski, Jeffrey J., Sheri Lynn Johnson, Andrew J. Wistrich, and Chris Guthrie. 2009. "Does Unconscious Racial Bias Affect Trial Judges?" *Notre Dame Law Review* 84(3): 1195–246.

Ramseyer, J. Mark. 1994. "The Puzzling (In)dependence of Courts: A Comparative Approach." *Journal of Legal Studies* 23(2): 721–47.

Ramseyer, J. Mark and Eric B. Rasmusen. 2006. "The Case for Managed Judges: Learning from Japan After the Political Upheaval of 1993." *University of Pennsylvania Law Review* 154(6): 1879–930.

Ramseyer, J. Mark and Eric B. Rasmussen. 2001. "Why Are Japanese Judges So Conservative in Politically Charged Cases?" *American Political Science Review* 95(2): 331–44.

Randazzo, Kirk A. 2008. "Strategic Anticipation and the Hierarchy of Justice in the U.S. District Courts." *American Politics Research* 36(5): 669–93.

Reichman, Amnon. 2013. Judicial Constitution Making in a Divided Society. In *Consequential Courts*, eds. Diana Kapiszewski, Gordon Silverstein, and Robert A. Kagan. Cambridge: Cambridge University Press.

Rice, Douglas R. and Christopher Zorn. 2021. "Corpus-Based Dictionaries for Sentiment Analysis of Specialized Vocabularies." *Political Science Research and Methods* 9(1): 20–35.

Richman, Barak D., Mario Bergara, and Pablo T. Spiller. 2003. "Modeling Supreme Court Strategic Decision Making: The Congressional Constraint." *Legislative Studies Quarterly* 28(2): 247–80.

Robinson, Nick. 2013. "Structure Matters: The Impact of Court Structure on the Indian and U.S. Supreme Courts." *American Journal of Comparative Law* 61(1): 173–208.

Rohde, David W. 1972. "Policy Goals and Opinion Coalitions in the Supreme Court." *Midwest Journal of Political Science* 16(2): 208–24.

Rosenberg, Gerald N. 1992. "Judicial Independence and the Reality of Political Power." *Review of Politics* 54(3): 369–98.

Rosenberg, Gerald N, Sudhir Krishnaswamy, and Shishir Bail, eds. 2019. *A Qualified Hope: The Indian Supreme Court and Progressive Social Change*. Cambridge: Cambridge University Press.

Salamone, Michael F. 2018. *Perceptions of a Polarized Court: How Division Among Justices Shapes the Supreme Court's Public Image*. Philadelphia, PA: Temple University Press.

Salzberger, Eli and Paul Fenn. 1999. "Judicial Independence: Some Evidence from the English Court of Appeal." *Journal of Law and Economics* 42(2): 831–47.

Schauer, Frederick. 2000. "Incentives, Reputation, and the Inglorious Determinants of Judicial Behavior." *University of Cincinnati Law Review* 68(3): 615–36.

Schelling, Thomas C. 1960. *The Strategy of Conflict*. Cambridge, MA: Harvard University Press.

Schubert, Glendon and David J. Danelski, eds. 1969. *Comparative Judicial Behavior*. New York: Oxford University Press.

Segal, Jeffrey A., Avani Mehta Sood, and Benjamin Woodson. 2018. "The 'Murder-Scene Exception' – Myth or Reality? Empirically Testing the Influence of Crime Severity in Federal Search-and-Seizure Cases." *Virginia Law Review* 105(3): 543–94.

Segal, Jeffrey A. and Harold J. Spaeth. 2002. *The Supreme Court and the Attitudinal Model Revisited*. Cambridge: Cambridge University Press.

Segal, Jeffrey A., Chad Westerland, and Stephanie Lindquist. 2011. "Congress, the Supreme Court, and Judicial Review: Testing a Constitutional Separation of Powers Model." *American Journal of Political Science* 55(1): 89–104.

Sen, Maya. 2015. "Is Justice Really Blind? Race and Appellate Review in U.S. Courts." *Journal of Legal Studies* 44(S1): 187–229.

Shapiro, Sidney A. and Richard E. Levy. 1995. "Judicial Incentives and Indeterminacy in Substantive Review of Administrative Decisions." *Duke Law Journal* 44(6): 1051–80.

Shayo, Moses and Asaf Zussman. 2011. "Judicial Ingroup Bias in the Shadow of Terrorism." *Quarterly Journal of Economics* 126(3): 1447–84.

Sill, Kaitlyn L. and Stacia L. Haynie. 2010. "Panel Assignment in Appellate Courts: Strategic Behaviour in the South African Supreme Court of Appeal." *Politikon* 37(2): 269–85.

Silverstein, Gordon. 2008. Singapore: The Exception that Proves Rules Matter. In *Rule by Law: The Politics of Courts in Authoritarian Regimes*, eds. Tom Ginsburg and Tamir Moustafa. Cambridge: Cambridge University Press.

Simon, Dan and Nicholas Scurich. 2013. "Judicial Overstating." *Chicago-Kent Law Review* 88(2): 411–31.

Sisk, Gregory C., Michael Heise, and Andrew P. Morriss. 2004. "Searching for the Soul of Judicial Decisionmaking: An Empirical Study of Religious Freedom Decision." *Ohio State Law Journal* 65(3): 491–614.

Snidal, Duncan. 1986. The Game *Theory* of International Politics. In *Cooperation Under Anarchy*, ed. Kenneth A. Oye. Princeton, NJ: Princeton University Press.

Sommer, Udi. 2010. "A Strategic Court and National Security: Comparative Lessons from the Israeli Case." *Israel Studies Review* 25(2): 54–80.

Songer, Donald R., Jeffrey A. Segal, and Charles M. Cameron. 1994. "The Hierarchy of Justice: Testing a Principal-Agent Theory of Supreme Court-Circuit Court Interactions." *Journal of Politics* 38(3): 673–96.

Sonnemans, Joep and Frans van Dijk. 2012. "Errors in Judicial Decisions: Experimental Results." *Journal of Law, Economics, and Organization* 28(4): 687–716.

Spamann, Holger and Lars Klohn. 2016. "Justice is Less Blind, and Less Legalistic, Than We Thought: Evidence from an Experiment with Real Judges." *Journal of Legal Studies* 45(2): 255–80.

Spiller, Pablo T. and Rafael Gely. 1992. "Congressional Control or Judicial Independence: The Determinants of U.S. Supreme Court Labor-Relation Decisions." *RAND Journal of Economics* 23(4): 463–92.

Spiller, Pablo T. and Emerson H. Tiller. 1996. "Invitations to Override: Congressional Reversals of Supreme Court Decisions." *International Review of Law and Economics* 16(4): 503–21.

Spitzer, Matt and Eric Talley. 2000. "Judicial Auditing." *Journal of Legal Studies* 29(2): 649–83.

Spriggs, James F., II, Forrest Maltzman, and Paul J. Wahlbeck. 1999. "Bargaining on the U.S. Supreme Court: Justices' Responses to Majority Opinion Drafts." *Journal of Politics* 61(2): 485–506.

Spriggs, James F., II and Paul J. Wahlbeck. 1997. "Amicus Curiae and the Role of Information at the Supreme Court." *Political Research Quarterly* 50(2): 365–86.

Squire, Peverill. 1988. "Politics and Personal Factors in Retirement from the United States Supreme Court." *Political Behavior* 10(2): 180–90.

Staton, Jeffrey K. 2010. *Judicial Power and Strategic Communication in Mexico*. New York: Cambridge University Press.

Staton, Jeffrey K. and Georg Vanberg. 2008. "The Value of Vagueness: Delegation, Defiance, and Judicial Opinions." *American Journal of Political Science* 52(3): 504–19.

Stephenson, Matthew C. 2003. "'When the Devil Turns . . . ': The Political Foundations of Independent Judicial Review." *Journal of Legal Studies* 32(1): 59–89.

Sternberg, Sebastian. 2018. "Why Do Courts Craft Vague Decisions? Evidence from a Comparative Study of Court Rulings in Germany and France Using Quantitative Text Analysis," University of Mannheim, Working Paper, available at https://sebastiansternberg.github.io/pdf/Sternberg_Value_of_Vagueness_CEL SE18.pdf.

Stewart, Pamela and Anita Stuhmcke. 2020. "Judicial Analytics and Australian Courts: A Call for National Ethical Guidelines." *Alternative Law Journal* 45(2): 82–7.

Stone, Alec. 1995. Complex Coordinate Construction in France and Germany. In *The Global Expansion of Judicial Power*, eds. C. Neal Tate and Torbjörn Vallinder. New York: New York University Press.

Sweet, Alec Stone. and Thomas L. Brunell. 1998. "The European Court and the National Courts: A Statistical Analysis of Preliminary References." *Journal of European Public Policy* 5(1): 66–97.

Tate, C. Neal. 1971. "The Social Background, Political Recruitment, and Decision-making of the Philippine Supreme Court." PhD Thesis, Tulane University.

Thaler, Richard H. 2015. *Misbehaving: The Making of Behavior Economics*. New York: Norton.

Toma, Eugenia Froedge. 1991. "Congressional Influence and the Supreme Court: The Budget as a Signaling Device." *Journal of Legal Studies* 20(1): 131–46.

Vanberg, Georg. 2005. *The Politics of Constitutional Review in Germany*. Cambridge: Cambridge University Press.

Vanberg, Georg. 2015. "Constitutional Courts in Comparative Perspective: A Theoretical Assessment." *Annual Review of Political Science* 18: 167–85.

Velicogna, Marco and Gar Yein Ng. 2006. "Legitimacy and Internet in the Judiciary: A Lesson From the Italian Courts' Websites Experience." *International Journal of Law and Information Technology* 14(3): 370–89.

Vining, Richard L., Susan Navarro Smelcer, and Christopher J. Zorn. 2006. "Judicial Tenure on the U.S. Supreme Court, 1790–1868: Frustration, Resignation, and Expiration on the Bench." *Studies in American Political Development* 20(2): 198–210.

Voeten, Erik. 2008. "The Impartiality of International Judges: Evidence from the European Court of Human Rights." *American Political Science Review* 102(4): 417–33.

Voeten, Erik. 2010. "Borrowing and Nonborrowing among International Courts." *Journal of Legal Studies* 39(2): 547–76.

Voeten, Erik. 2020. "Populism and Backlashes against International Courts." *Perspectives on Politics*, 18(2): 407–22.

Vunikili, Ramya, Hitesh Ochani, Divisha Jaiswal et al. 2018. "Analysis of Vocal Implicit Bias in Scotus Decisions Through Predictive Modelling," available at https://ssrn.com/abstract=3307296.

Weiden, David L. 2011. "Judicial Politicization, Ideology, and Activism at the High Courts of the United States, Canada, and Australia." *Political Research Quarterly* 64(2): 335–47.

Weinshall, Keren and Lee Epstein. 2020. "Developing High-Quality Data Infrastructure for Legal Analytics: Introducing the Israeli Supreme Court Database." *Journal of Empirical Legal Studies*, 17(2): 416–34.

Weinshall, Keren, Udi Sommer, and Ya'acov Ritov. 2018. "Ideological Influences on Governance and Regulation: The Comparative Case of Supreme Courts." *Regulation & Governance* 12(3): 334–52.

Weinshall-Margel, Keren. 2011. "Attitudinal and Neo-Institutional Models of Supreme Court Decision Making: An Empirical and Comparative Perspective from Israel." *Journal of Empirical Legal Studies* 8(3): 556–86.

Westerland, Chad, Jeffrey A. Segal, Lee Epstein, Charles Cameron, and Scott Comparato. 2010. "Strategic Defiance and Compliance in the U.S. Courts of Appeals." *American Journal of Political Science* 54(4): 891–905.

Wetstein, Matthew E., C. L. Ostberg, Donald R. Songer, and Susan W. Johnson. 2009. "Ideological Consistency and Attitudinal Conflict: A Comparative Analysis of the U.S. and Canadian Supreme Courts." *Comparative Political Studies* 42(6): 753–92.

Wistrich, Andrew J., Jeffrey J. Rachlinski, and Chris Guthrie. 2015. "Heart Versus Head: Do Judges Follow the Law or Follow Their Feelings." *Texas Law Review* 93(4): 855–923.

Zorn, Christopher and Jennifer Barnes Bowie. 2010. "Ideological Influences on Decision Making in the Federal Judicial Hierarchy: An Empirical Assessment." *Journal of Politics* 72(4): 1212–21.

Acknowledgments

Lee Epstein is the Ethan A.H. Shepley Distinguished University Professor at Washington University in St. Louis; Keren Weinshall is the Edward S. Silver Chair in Civil Procedure and Vice-Dean of the Faculty of Law at Hebrew University of Jerusalem. Epstein thanks the John Simon Guggenheim Foundation, the National Science Foundation, and Washington University for supporting her research on judicial behavior. Weinshall thanks the Israel Science Foundation (grant no. 1404/17). Because this Element is a substantially revised version of Epstein and Jacobi (2010) and draws on Epstein and Knight (2018), we thank Tonja Jacobi and Jack Knight for their contributions. We are also very grateful to the editors and the anonymous reviewers for their thoughtful and helpful comments.

Cambridge Elements ≡

Law, Economics and Politics

Series Editor in Chief
Carmine Guerriero, *University of Bologna*

Series Co-Editors
Rosa Ferrer, *UPF and Barcelona GSE*
Nuno Garoupa, *George Mason University*
Mariana Mota Prado, *University of Toronto*
Murat Mungan, *George Mason University*

Series Managing Editor
Liam Wells, *Erasmus University, Rotterdam*

Series Associate Editors
Tim Friehe, *Philipps-Universität Marburg*
Marie Obidzinski, *Université Paris 2*
Anna Bindler, *University of Cologne*
Jo Seldeslachts, *University of Amsterdam*
Andy Hanssen, *Clemson University*
Sara Biancini, *Université de Cergy-Pontoise*
Pedro Magalhães, *ICS, Lisbon*
Kelly Rader, *Yale University*
Jed Kroncke, *Hong Kong University*
Sara Ghebremusse, *University of British Columbia*

About the Series
Individual decision-making is influenced by formal rules (including laws), legal and political 'institutions', and 'informal institutions' influenced by social norms. These institutions determine the nature, scope and operation of markets, organisations and states. This interdisciplinary series analyses the functioning, determinants and impact of these institutions, organizing the existing knowledge and guiding future research.

Cambridge Elements ≡

Law, Economics and Politics

Elements in the Series

Printed in the United States
by Baker & Taylor Publisher Services